Improving Your
Students' Learning

Open and Distance Learning Series

Series Editor: Fred Lockwood

Improving Your Students' Learning

Reflections on the Experience of Study

ALISTAIR MORGAN

KOGAN PAGE
Published in association with the
Institute of Educational Technology, Open University

London • Philadelphia

First published in 1993

Kogan Page Limited
120 Pentonville Road
London N1 9JN

British Library Cataloguing in Publication Data

A CIP record for this book is available from the British Library

ISBN 0 7494 0712 3

Typeset by BookEns Limited, Baldock, Herts.
Printed and bound in Great Britain by Biddles Ltd, Guildford and Kings Lynn.

Contents

Series editor's foreword

The use of open and distance learning is increasing dramatically in all sections of education and training, both in the UK and around the world. Many schools, colleges, universities, companies and organizations are already using open and distance learning practices in their teaching and training and want to develop these further. Furthermore, many individuals have heard about open and distance learning and would welcome the opportunity to find out more about it and explore its potential.

Whatever your current interest in open and distance learning and experience within it, I believe there will be something in this series of short books for you. This series is directed at teachers, trainers, educational advisers, in-house training managers and training consultants involved in designing open and distance learning systems and materials. It will be invaluable for those working in learning environments ranging from industry and commerce to public sector organizations, from schools and colleges to universities.

This series is designed to provide a comprehensive coverage of the field of open and distance learning. Each title focuses on a different aspect of designing and developing open and distance learning and provides concrete advice and information, which is built upon current theory and research in the field and how it relates to actual practice. This basis, of theory, research and development experience, is unique in the area of open and distance learning. I say this with some confidence since the Open University Institute of Educational Technology, from which virtually all the authors are drawn, contains the largest collection of educational technologists (course designers, developers and researchers) in the world. Since the inception of the Open University in 1969 members of the Institute have made a major contribution to the design and production of learning systems and materials, not just in the Open University, but in many other organizations in the UK and many countries around the world. We would now like to share our experience and findings with you.

In this book, *Improving Your Students' Learning: Reflections on the Experience of Study*, Alistair Morgan describes research in student learning drawn from the Open University and other open and distance learning contexts, as well as from conventional educational settings. The aim of the book is to present the learners' experiences of learning as a basis for 'critical reflection' on the practice of teaching and learning. Although this book is based on research, it is presented in an accessible way, so as to raise teachers', trainers' and course designers' awareness of students' experiences of learning. This understanding of the learner's experience is presented as a vitally important aspect of theorizing practice and improving the quality of learning. Throughout the book, the aim is to draw research, theory and practice into a closer relationship, so as to encourage teachers and trainers to become 'reflective practitioners' in their efforts to change and improve their own practices of teaching and learning.

Fred Lockwood

Acknowledgements

In writing this book, I must acknowledge my former colleagues Liz Beaty and Graham Gibbs for the collaborative work in the Study Methods Group in the Institute of Educational Technology (IET) at the Open University. (The Study Methods Group was a Research Group in IET prior to the departmental reorganization which established the Student Research Centre.) Much of the research with OU students was carried out by the Study Methods Group and this book owes a lot to this work with Beaty and Gibbs. I must thank Liz for permission to use some extracts from her PhD thesis in Chapter 2 and for some of the ideas about orientation to education (she is cited by her former name, Taylor.) I also express thanks to Graham for permission to use the examples of caricatures of different styles of lecturers in Chapter 3.

I would also like to acknowledge support and encouragement from IET colleagues Derek Rowntree, Nick Farnes and Clive Lawless, who have commented on some of the chapters, as well as the Series Editor, Fred Lockwood. I want to thank Ference Marton for the encouragement he provided when we started to use some of his ideas for understanding student learning in the OU. I am also indebted to Malcolm Parlett for numerous discussions and suggestions when he was Visiting Professor here in IET.

I owe special thanks to Sue Gibbons for her support and encouragement, and also for critically commenting on some of the material.

Finally, I express thanks to Willy Russell and Methuen, London, for permission to use the extract from *Educating Rita* in Chapter 5, and also to David Lodge and Martin Secker and Warburg for permission to use the extract from *Changing Places* in Chapter 5.

Introduction

The aim of this book is to describe students' experiences of learning, in a range of education and training settings. The basic tenet of this book is that understanding learning from the learners' perspective is the crucial starting point for our work as teachers, trainers and course designers in improving student learning in distance and open learning. This may seem a rather obvious, common-sense and uncontentious issue. However, I believe much of the debate about teaching and learning is focused on the content, with insufficient attention given to how students attempt to study and understand it. Developing course content is one of our major tasks, but I want to put the student's experience 'centre stage', as a significant dimension to improving student learning.

In this book, I want to raise the critical issues for teachers, trainers and course designers in open and distance learning, as well as in conventional educational settings, of the 'how', 'what' and 'why' of the experience of being a student – surviving as a student if you like. The book is based on research and evaluation of student learning carried out in the UK, Sweden, Australia and the USA in both higher education and the vocational training sector, with students studying with open and distance learning and also in conventional education settings. The aim is to suggest how our practice might be improved by an understanding of research. The book is steeped in research, but this is presented in an accessible way to raise the awareness of 'being a student', so that you can consider what this means for your own students. I believe that raising the awareness of the learner's experience is fundamental to addressing change in our teaching and learning practice. This raises questions about the relationships between research, theory and practice. Also it raises fundamental issues about the way we operate in practice, as professionals, and especially, how do we *change* our practice?

In understanding learning from the learner's perspective, there are five closely interrelated focuses:

- Orientation to education
- Conceptions of learning
- Approaches to learning
- Outcomes of learning and students' change and development
- Organizational constraints and the assessment system

The book explores these five dimensions of the students' experiences. In terms of how we change our practice and how as professionals we respond to understanding the learners' perspective, I want to locate this work within a framework of 'critical reflection'.

My aim is to present a holistic understanding of studying, when viewed from the learner's perspective, in the hope that it will stimulate your reflection on your own practice in open and distance learning and initiate change. This book is concerned with *change* from the learner's perspective and also *change* in the organizational context. In Chapter 1, change from the learner's perspective is introduced by looking at an autobiography of a hypothetical student from the foundation year through to graduation. This account of one student's experience maps out the critical issues for student learning, which are developed in the subsequent chapters.

Chapter 2 discusses students' 'orientations to education' – a sort of 'holistic motivation' – which describes how students come to be engaged in education and training. The aims, aspirations and purposes which students have in studying have a major impact on how they tackle their studies. In terms of improving student learning, we need to become more aware of the diversity of students' purposes, and at the same time to encourage students to become more reflective themselves.

In Chapters 3 and 4, the detailed processes of how students tackle their studies are discussed. Chapter 3 looks at how learning and understanding are the crucial issues for education and training at all levels. Then there is a description of how research into students' conceptions of learning has identified a number of key distinctions between students. Students' conceptions of learning are vitally important in terms of improving learning, as these appear to have a limiting influence on 'what' students actually do in their studies. Chapter 4 continues the discussion on 'approaches to learning' and explores the key distinction between a deep and a surface approach to learning. In terms of improving student learning, how do certain aspects of course design influence and change the ways students study? There is a discussion of the scope for 'interventions' by teachers and trainers in terms of course design to improve learning.

Chapter 5 moves to understanding the organizational context of learning by addressing the question, 'What are students supposed to learn?' The debate looks at how certain aspects of the assessment system can have unintended 'side-effects' and can easily induce students to adopt a surface approach to learning. What types of change at the organizational level can teachers, trainers and course designers make to facilitate student learning? The approach of 'critical reflection' is discussed here in more detail. Throughout the book, we are essentially looking at ways of understanding complex issues of learning, and at the same time critically reflecting with this knowledge in terms of change, and with the aim of identifying obstacles and barriers to change.

In Chapter 6 the outcomes of learning are looked at in detail. How do students describe their gains from education and training? In what ways have their understanding of key concepts developed. Besides looking at the content of learning in terms of conceptual change, there is a discussion of students' development as learners and how they develop skill in learning. Also this chapter looks at the gains and changes from education and training in a wider social and political context by exploring some of the interactions of study in open and distance learning with people's lives.

The Conclusion draws together the summaries and conclusions of the chapters, so as to emphasize the implications of understanding the learners' perspective for fostering a deep approach to learning and thus improving your students' learning.

Chapter 1

One student's experiences: from first year to graduation

Introduction

Why should you pay attention to one student's experiences? In this fictional autobiographical account, I want to provide the opportunity for you to reflect on the experience of being a student, and to relate the issues to your own situation. Although the student referred to here is engaged in full-time post-compulsory education, the issues raised are relevant to students engaged in open learning or distance education on a part-time basis. The relevance of the insights from this student's experience is particularly pertinent at a time when conventional universities are increasingly adopting self-instructional or distance learning materials and when the boundaries between different sectors in post-compulsory education are rapidly becoming blurred. The conventional boundaries between education and training are also changing rapidly, hence the significance of drawing together the crucial issues of improving quality in open and distance learning in the widest sense. The aim of this chapter is to raise your awareness as a teacher, trainer or course designer of the 'how, what and why' of the experiences of being a student. Also by using a conventional educational setting as a starting point, there may well be more parallels to your own experiences of being a student in post-compulsory education. This chapter will also introduce the key themes for understanding student learning which are developed in the subsequent chapters.

The first steps

Towards the end of my first year in the lower 6th form, with A-level examinations in the following year, we had a session with the careers master about the options for higher education.

'OK, you lot', he asked, 'who wants to go to university?'

I put my hand up with about four other members of our class of about twenty. I suppose I'm up to it, I thought. My sister went to Durham, and my father did an External London Degree by part-time study; my parents seem to expect me to go to university, so I might as well, I thought – three years of having a good time seemed quite appealing.

'Is that all?' our careers master remarked in amazement.

A few more people, seeing the support of this initial group, also raised their hands, but without much idea of what they might be letting themselves in for.

'Fine, that's a better number,' our careers master commented, obviously with an eye for the school track record on university entrants. 'You can collect the clearing house application forms from my office and you'd better decide what subjects you want to do fairly soon. Come to see me if you want to talk more about it.'

[I appreciate that the quality of careers guidance and counselling has improved dramatically from the type of session just mentioned.]

So what subjects should we do? Might as well carry on doing our best subjects, we agreed as a group. One of these science subjects: it would be quite trendy to be a scientist. Right, I'd go for physics.

So, off I went to university to study physics. It was an interesting subject, which I had found pretty straightforward at school. Looking back after almost thirty years, I'm not suggesting that I was pushed into this subject, by school or by parents. I suppose it sort of happened to me – the next step on the academic ladder.

The transition from school to university was shattering. Nobody really seemed to care about me and the problems I was experiencing. So much new information was being presented to me, and coping with lectures as a main teaching method after the more supportive tutorial style at school was particularly difficult. I found it really difficult to handle the very different styles of lectures from various members of the teaching staff.

For instance, one lecturer wrote up all the material on the blackboard, and gave us reasonable time to copy it all down into our notes. He made it pretty clear that his lectures would cover all that we needed for the examinations. The notes I managed to take in these lectures were quite neat and orderly, there was no need to do any rewriting. Just copying down all the content of lectures was fine, as then I could start the task of trying to remember all this new information. One of the post-graduate students who worked as a laboratory demonstrator described lectures as 'just a vehicle for transmitting the lecturer's notes to the students' notes, without either party really thinking about anything!' Some of the lectures certainly felt a bit like that, but at least I got good notes which made some sense when I started revision.

Another lecturer seemed to take a totally different approach. He based his teaching around three set books. He claimed that his lectures were going to 'weave together the content of the books for us and to clarify the more difficult concepts'. A fine idea, but I found it very difficult to know what to do about taking notes. Sometimes the material he wrote on the board was extremely clear and understandable, better than the set books, but in many places he went off at a tangent and brought in his own research interests, which few us were able to understand. His enthusiasm for telling us about his research seemed to blind him from seeing the fifty or so bored expressions! Every time I looked over the notes I took in those lectures I kept wishing he would tell us what to learn, or help us 'to see the wood from the trees' in all this new material.

Apart from a small number of tutorials, the teaching methods seemed to be rather conventional and just following the established pattern with lectures being the predominant approach to teaching. However, I do have some recollections of one teaching 'experiment' from a relatively new member of staff, who had recently been on a course on teaching and learning in higher education. He was very keen to try out ideas from programmed learning and self-instructional teaching texts. Consequently, the class was divided into two groups and one group received three lectures on the particular topic and the other group worked independently on the self-instructional text. At the end of this teaching, after three weeks, both groups were required to complete the same test in an attempt to compare the effectiveness of the two teaching methods. The results showed that there was no significant difference between them. The most revealing finding was the dismally poor performance from all of us in both groups. Nobody seemed to have learnt very much at all!

Probably the most important conclusion from this little experiment was that the complexities of teaching and learning are not easily reduced to the experimental manipulations of physical science. Comparing teaching methods is not quite so straightforward as comparing the efficiency of different agricultural fertilisers! Also, as students we were not as easily manipulated by teaching devices in self-instructional texts as our teacher and the enthusiastic course designer or educational technologist would like to believe!

I found coping with the demands of university level study difficult and the college appeared to offer little in the way of support or guidance to help me. The so-called personal tutor in the faculty wasn't very helpful. In fact, I regarded him as an arrogant and rather pompous twit! I'm sure his academic credentials were very good, but empathy with students and his listening skills were not his strong points. The nearest he could get to understanding my problems was to give a monologue about himself as an undergraduate at Cambridge, and how things were just going to be tough. Nobody seemed to care if I was heading for failure and also there seemed to be a large core of people who were brighter than me, or at least seemed to be coping better. Many of the teaching staff appeared to be somewhat uninterested in first year students, as if they were a diversion from their real interests of specialist teaching and research. So the start of my university career was not very impressive.

Another aspect of coping with university study that I vividly recall was laboratory work. The first laboratory report I submitted was quite good in my opinion. I had worked hard at it, doing the best I could, based on experiences at school. Alas, it came back with a borderline pass mark written on it, and the comments also implied that the grade was rather generous. Things were not looking good now. Perhaps I wasn't cut out for university study after all. Quite a shock really, when school work for O-level and A-level had appeared fairly straightforward. By chance the demonstrator, a postgraduate student, was very helpful in showing me what sort of thing to do in the future. So for the next practical work I tried to do it differently. Besides the amazingly time-consuming experimental work, I tried to look critically at the experiment in relation to the relevant theory. What were the sources of error? How else could the measurement be made? How could the experimental equipment be redesigned to provide a more valuable set of data in relation to the research question and the aims of the laboratory class? Although I had put in far more effort than on the first occasion, I was still unsure about what I had written. So I was quite anxious to find out how my work had been received. To my surprise and trepidation, there was a note summoning me to see the professor in charge of the first year. Was this to be even harsher comment on my work? Or what? To my surprise, this professor had my laboratory report in front of him.

'I want to talk to you about your practical work,' he remarked, by way of introduction. As he passed the report back to me, I could see the comments, 'A+ Excellent Work'. He continued, 'This is the best piece of work I have seen from that experiment; and I wanted to talk to you about what you have done and also to ask your permission to keep a copy of your report for the department library, as it contains some original ideas.' I naturally agreed to the material being copied and felt quite elated. Perhaps I was beginning to understand what undergraduate physics was about, or at least in the area of one piece of laboratory work.

In spite of this glimmer of success, the first year experience was difficult. Besides the turmoil of the social and sexual development, there was a gradual awareness that I was doing the wrong subject. My interests in the environmental sciences, that I was taking as a subsidiary subject, were start-ing to get my main attention. 'I've got to change course,' I said to myself. That became my main aim for my second term of undergraduate study.

How had my interest in physics diminished? First, I probably drifted into the subject, just following on from school. Second, I was becoming more aware of the social and political aspects of science, of values and ideologies. Surprisingly, these issues seemed to be absent in the first-year physics course. And third, the way the subject was presented in the environmental science department seemed to be different. Or perhaps it was the style and ethos of the department which was different. The lectures were of a more interesting style; besides set presentations, there were discussion activities, to help us to sort out what we were gaining from a lecture. The staff seemed to be genuinely concerned to help students to learn, rather than 'to set hurdles for us and to watch our progress or lack of it', which seemed to be more of the style in the physics department.

The subsidiary courses in the environmental sciences seemed to me to be more interesting. There appeared to be less of a body of fact that we were being told to assimilate, in contrast to the way physics was being taught to us, at least at first year level. The teachers in environmental sciences seemed to appreciate a diversity of interests among us, perhaps due to the more interdisciplinary nature of their field. Anyway, I became convinced that I had to change course, even though it was over half way through the first year.

Changing courses

So I was committed to the idea of changing my subject to environmental sciences. But how to do it? There was certainly no mention of changing courses in the guide to applicants, or the faculty prospectus, or the glossy brochures about the college. I had a vague notion that some universities and polytechnics had broad common core courses in the first year, prior to later specialization. Surely my idea couldn't be totally stupid, or impossible to achieve? A tutor in the physics department, whom I had got to know quite well through non-academic activities, namely mountaineering, thought it would be possible to change, but probably at the end of the first year. He introduced me to a senior member of staff in environmental sciences to talk 'hypothetically' about changing course.

The new department seemed to welcome the idea. After a number of meetings, it was agreed that I would change at the end of first year, but only after the physics department had made a final bid to keep me in their patch. As the admissions tutor in physics commented, 'What did you expect from first year study? There are all these facts you have to learn before you can start to do the interesting things.'

They were clearly not at all keen or helpful about me changing courses. They showed me a project report from a final year student in an attempt to get me to reconsider changing. It was too late. I was convinced about changing and started to look forward to the next year. However there was one difficulty. This change was conditional on my passing the first year examinations to fulfil the university regulations. This was a dreadful prospect. I had to study and revise for a subject area I was going to give up.

If I wanted to pursue my interests, that was what I was going to have to do. So I just looked at the task of finishing the first year in a purely mechanistic way. I scanned through the old examination papers, to get some idea of the type of questions asked and also attempted to do some 'question spotting'. I also managed to extract a few hints from a junior lecturer in the physics department, whom I now knew quite well through mountaineering.

Replying to a somewhat facetious question I put to him in the bar, 'What's coming up in the exams then?' he claimed to have absolutely no detailed knowledge of the first year examination papers. However, there was also a rather guarded remark about 'certain things not to worry about too much', in the form, 'such and such a professor's lectures don't really matter for first year exams'. Then I set out to memorize a few set formulae and equations which seemed to come up regularly in past papers and hoped to scrape through. I succeeded in passing! The right questions came up for the material which I had committed to memory. I'd done as well as I needed. I'd passed the first year and was now going on to study environmental sciences. Besides being a year older, I'd learnt quite a bit about myself in the process of changing course. I started to become more aware of how I came to be at university, and a better understanding of my own interests.

Sharing experiences

I always found it helpful, especially in times of uncertainty, to find out how friends made sense of being at college. I was always keen to explore such issues and to share experiences during chats in the bar or over coffee. However, many of my friends thought I was stupid to be changing course. 'You're going to have to work so hard to catch up all that material you have missed during the first year,' was a typical remark. 'If you don't manage it you'll fail at the end of the second year, and you will have wasted two years of your life,' was another one.

I thought some of this was jealousy about making a bold decision.

One quite close friend was studying Business Administration with the aim of working in that field. His sole aim in being at university seemed to be to gain the training to go into the family business and also to get the degree. His parents owned and ran a medium-sized engineering company, and he was essentially being trained to carry on the family business. Although his first year had seemed irrelevant to his needs for some basic training, he felt obliged to persevere. Two things seemed to drive him in this direction: his parents had such strong expectations that their son would follow in the family tradition; and also he would have a secure job to go to on graduation. So he was going to stick it out; it was only another two years.

Other friends had arrived at university with very different aims and aspirations. One had 'a sort of country club' notion of the university. She had been at school in a university town. She had seen the social side of college life and quite liked the idea of spending three years in a similar way. The regulations required her to register in a faculty, so she had opted for her best subject at school. Although she found this boring, she could fulfil the assessment requirements of gaining a bare pass without too much bother. Her main interests were in student union activities and she became editor of the student newspaper. I felt quite envious of her confidence in pursuing her own interests, which were essentially tangential to the official aims of the university. She was not bound by the rigid demands of the syllabus. Rather, it was a means to an end, enabling her to follow her own interests.

Here's how another of my friends was trying to make sense and survive in the course of his original choice. He did not like his course and thought he had chosen the wrong subject, but reacted in a very different way from me. I had struggled a bit to explore the options for changing courses and had managed that in the end. This friend, however, just seemed content to stick it out to get a degree. He had some vague notions of going into management training, where the initial degree did not seem to be very important. So he made a clear decision to finish the course by the easiest possible route, essentially, by concentrating on the minimum that could be memorized for the examinations, a bit like the way I had approached the first year.

Back in the second year

In the second year, in the environmental sciences department, it was certainly hard work to catch up on the material I had missed, in spite of my studies over the long vacation. But the nature of my effort seemed to have changed; the way I tackled a piece of work was different. I seemed to be more reflective in what I was doing. In so much of the first year, I just took study and learning for granted and I didn't stop to think about what I was really doing. I was rushing through material trying to remember it all and trying to get everything done.

In the second year, the way I used my time seemed to be different. I could stand back from the detail of individual pieces of work, and look at them critically. How did they relate to other material I had studied? What was this lecturer trying to communicate to us? What was it really about? Studying actually became quite fun as I was personally motivated in what I was doing. My whole attitude towards the university was different; a change to a much more intrinsic interest in the academic content of what I was doing and also towards possible vocational aspects in the future.

In many ways I had changed as a person. I had a lot more confidence in how to tackle various assignment tasks, particularly in understanding the demands of different pieces of work, which were part of the continuous assessment. It certainly paid to suss-out the interests of different members of staff, and how they marked and assessed our work. It was just part of the process of thinking more about what I was doing and how I was doing it.

Developing confidence: moving towards graduation.

At the end of the second year, after catching up and doing pretty well in the examinations, I developed a personal interest in the philosophy of science. I got particularly interested in the arguments about objectivity and subjectivity in science. Some of the writings on the subjectivity in science, on the uncertainties in the status of scientific knowledge, seemed to bear little relation to the way much of the teaching had been conducted in the university. The notion that the teaching staff knew all the 'answers' was the implicit message in the way the majority of lectures were given. Also many of the staff seemed to like to display themselves as the experts to be looked up to.

This reading outside the formal course requirements gave me a new 'lens' with which to examine what I was doing for the course. The idea of facts in environmental sciences started to look problematical, or at least not to be taken at face value. I suppose I was starting to see knowledge itself in a different way. Quite exciting really! Perhaps I was just becoming a different sort of person from the shy eighteen-year-old, straight from school, and looking up in awe at the university and its staff of learned experts! I guess things were beginning to appear more complicated than they had hitherto, but it seemed to be a more exciting world.

This reminds me of a series of lectures from visiting speakers at the start of the final year on theories of urban development. These formed part of the social science strand of the environmental science course. They were certainly quite difficult to understand, as the lecturers were talking about their research interests, almost as if they were addressing a conference or a group of post-graduate students. It was the content of these lectures that tended to dominate our tutorial discussions for a while, as some members of our tutorial group appeared to be confused.

Our tutor just got the tutorials going by asking what we had learnt from these lectures. 'What were the speakers trying to communicate to you?' As well as a way to initiate discussion, he was genuinely interested, as he had been unable to attend the lectures himself. One of the group broke the silence by admitting to having gone to sleep and not really understanding anything! It certainly generated some amusement. And then somebody else started off.

'Well it's about all these conflicting theories, as I see it. I suppose we just have to try to guess which one is the best one.'

'But do we have to choose one?' came from somebody else.

And again, the tutor was asked which one should be revised for the exam. He hesitated about answering. He was quite good at keeping us discussing without intervening too much. I remained silent though, not being quite able to articulate the position I wanted to put. Somebody else did this. She also seemed to gain the approval of the tutor.

'As I see it, you can't think of any theory being "right", you can only think in terms of its coherence and how you see the dominant forces in society shaping the nature of the urban environment. Social scientists disagree on this sort of thing, so it depends how you look at it. I think you have to be committed to a particular perspective in this field, and understand what that is based on.'

The rest of us were a bit silenced by her confidence. Some of the group were far from happy with that idea.

'OK, that's fine if you want to specialize in this field, but I'm still concerned about which theory is the best one to concentrate on for the examination,' came from another member of our group.

Our tutor now seemed to be in a difficult position, he couldn't really say anything to please everybody. I think we were all relieved when the time for the session had elapsed. As we dispersed, I overheard a few comments about 'woolly tutors' who don't tell you what to learn. However, this certainly wasn't my view of the tutorial, although in the first year I would have probably responded in a similar way.

I think this tutorial session brought together some of my reflections on learning and how my views had changed since the first year. I certainly didn't expect to be told exactly what to learn in the way that some of our tutorial group still seemed to expect. Quietly I think I was starting to see knowledge and learning in a different way. No longer was learning just about reproducing the content of the lecture notes, but rather, it was about putting things together and sort of 'constructing' meaning. I was certainly seeing the process of being a student in a very different way from in the first year. At that time, I don't think I ever stood back to examine what I was doing. It just all sort of happened to me.

The project work was probably the climax of the final year for me. It was so nice to be working on an activity for which the outcomes were not really clear. Quite a lot of the laboratory work we had done had been meant to help us understand techniques or demonstrate theoretical concepts. It had been reasonably interesting, but from the detail of the laboratory manuals, it was clear the activities had been run many times before. Some people almost treated them as 'cookery book' activities: just carry out the procedures as specified without really understanding what the experiment was about. By contrast, we were very much on our own for the projects. I found it great to be able to 'go it alone', and felt reasonably confident that I could produce some sort of report that would satisfy the examiners. True enough, the 'Big A' for assessment was still there, as it had been all the way through, but it didn't seem such a burden as earlier. And also the word around the department was that if you did a reasonable project, you would get a good degree. The regulations set out the criteria and grading scheme etc, but it was great to hear around the department that few people failed their projects, if they put in some real effort.

A close friend at home, who was also in her final year of a degree, was doing a project over the same time period, so we compared notes. She was doing an interdisciplinary modular course with lots of little components over a wide range of subject material – lots of choice, but perhaps not so much coherence. She described how some of her friends saw the gaining of module credits as a bit like 'stamp collecting'. When you had gained twenty-three credits (the stamps), you got a degree. Her project module counted for three credits. But it was her story about one of the traditionally taught modules, consisting of lectures, essays and an exam, which really got us sharing experiences about how dreadful some of the teaching is in post-compulsory education. In contrast, the project was an opportunity for 'real' learning. In her second year, in one module of just eight weeks, she reckoned she had started to revise for the exam after about week five of the course, before she had really come to understand any of the material. She described this as 'a bit scary really!' Again, this sort of learning experience is a direct consequence of the assessment system.

So how did my project work out? I enjoyed the freedom to be a more independent learner, and also on a more equal status with my project supervisor. As I became more immersed in the work, I actually came to know more about the details in the particular field than my supervisor, as I was more up to date with literature. Finishing off the project was a difficult task of focusing down and writing a coherent report. The main thing I recall was that it was 'my own piece of work', done by me. I was approaching the final exams. They only counted for half of the assessment, so the pressure was not too great. Also from the results of our project work, we had a fairly good idea how we were going to get on. It was quite tense, wondering what was going to come up, and trying to avoid feeling pressed into lots of last minute attempts to memorize material, but my study patterns had developed quite a lot since the first year, when I was trying to memorize a few facts and formulae. Well that was it. I passed the examinations and got an upper second! I was on course to get 'the piece of paper'. I was very pleased about that; to be getting a degree and the status attached to it, and the access to a certain form of discourse which a degree offers in our society. I had survived as a student, but my aims and purposes in study had changed dramatically over my career as an undergraduate.

Commentary

So, how do these experiences mirror your own? Have I triggered off ideas about yourself, or your undergraduate peers or more important, students you are currently teaching? What assessment requirements do you make of your students? How do these get decided? When did you last have a major review of the assessment system in your institution? The issues raised in this account of being a student are taken up in the following chapters. The overall aim of this book is to raise your awareness of the 'how, what and why' of 'being a student', so as to provide a basis for 'critical reflection' about teaching and learning in training and education and so to improve student learning.

By critical reflection, I am referring to the process of 'theorizing' our practices of teaching and training, to question its foundations and assumptions in a fundamental way. For example, 'What underlies student failure?' 'How is it that some students' submitted work is so dismal?' 'How is it that you teach your course in the way you do?' 'What are the constraints and barriers in experimenting with different forms of assessment?' 'What are your implicit theories of learning?' 'How do these influence the way you organize your courses?' 'Who controls the curriculum in your subject area and what access to this power do you have as an individual teacher or trainer?' And so on. Critical reflection is the process which enables us to become more aware of the contradictions and contestations which surround our education and training.

In the student's account above, the first key concept is 'orientation to education', or holistic motivation. This student ended up at university as a progression from school; it was the next step on the academic ladder, which 'happened' without much careful consideration of the other possibilities. In Chapter 2 we shall explain this as an 'academic extrinsic orientation to education'.

The change in course from physics to environmental sciences marks a change in orientation towards a more intrinsic orientation. Between the two courses, we can identify different ways in which the subject material is being tackled and also differences in the demands of the assessment. In order to gain a pass from the first year, our student in the fictional autobiography prepared for the exams by memorizing a few basic facts and formulae. He also seemed to be fairly 'cue-conscious' , from the way he 'button-holed' his mountaineering friend on the staff in the physics department, to get some hints about the examination questions.

In Chapters 3 and 4, the way the student actually tackles the learning activities is discussed by examining 'conceptions of learning', ie what students perceive learning to consist of, and 'approaches to learning', what students are attempting to do in their learning. In Chapter 5, we look at how students come to understand the demands of their courses through the assessment system.

Teaching and learning are intimately related to the student assessment procedures, so a crucial strand of the debate in Chapter 5 is how students find out what they are supposed to learn. At the same time, as teachers, trainers and course designers, how can we reflect critically on our assessment procedures as the basis for improving our practice?

Throughout this discussion, there will be an emphasis on 'change', as students progress from 'novices' engaged in their foundation level courses towards graduation and development as independent learners. Chapter 6 looks at learning outcomes and gains from study, and specifically at these overall changes and how students develop their skill and competence as learners.

In the following chapters we shall develop the key concepts for understanding learning, which are firmly grounded in students' realities of learning. This conceptual framework can be used in practice both to 'interrogate' the case of the hypothetical autobiographical account and more significantly, to form the basis for critical reflection on students' experiences in open learning and distance education in general.

As you consider your own education and training, what sorts of issues would come up in biographical sketches of your own students? What insights would these provide into your own teaching and about your own institutional practices?

Chapter 2
How do students come to be studying?

Introduction

As teachers, trainers and course designers, how do we talk about our learners? How do we describe the differences between them and how is it that there are great variations in performance in their studies? Very often the language used will refer to students being cleverer, keener, or more hardworking, or more intelligent. Similarly, within the student culture, there is a language for describing variations between people. The swots, the hardworking plodders and the 'really bright' people, who cruise through college, gaining high grades without appearing to do very much work. In the cases where students are only admitted to college on the basis of A-level performance (or equivalent examination), they have all demonstrated their ability to meet certain academic criteria. However, there is a low correlation between A-level grades and final degree results. Some institutions, for example the Open University (OU), admit mature students into the undergraduate programme with no formal entry qualifications. Hence some of the meaning of 'openness' implied in the name of the Open University. In fact in the OU, just under half the students have O-levels or less as their background qualifications and of these about a third progress to graduation. Increasingly mature students are being admitted to higher education on the basis of less formal qualifications. From the early 1990s much greater attention is being given to students' prior learning experiences and the assessment of prior learning.

Motivation is often used to explain differences in performance, but motivation is a poorly defined concept and difficult to measure. Attempts to develop measures of motivation and to correlate them with performance have not shown any clear patterns. At the intuitive level, a certain degree of hard work and application would seem to be necessary for success in university level education. However, this conceals the differences to do with the nature of this 'hard work' and how it is actually focused. Again researchers have had little success in correlating 'good' study habits with success at university. But what is to be defined as success? Is it just the accumulation of appropriate course credits and a formal qualification? This is clearly an important goal, but not the only outcome of university, whether from full time study in a conventional university, or on a part-time basis, taking the opportunities of open and distance learning. In our discussions of the aims of university education, we are concerned with more than the extrinsic goals of gaining certificates and the training of a skilled workforce.

Students have to *choose* to engage in post-compulsory education and training, at university or elsewhere, although for many students in their late teens there may be very great pressures from parents and school (or sixth form college) on them to enter higher education. By exploring students' perspectives for becoming engaged in education and training, we shall be in a better position to understand the variations in the students' performance. Some of these variations have already been highlighted in the case of our fictitious student in Chapter 1.

Why study? Students' views

I want to explore the issues raised above by looking at the cases of some real students. A number of research studies (Taylor, Morgan and Gibbs, 1981; Taylor, 1983; Gibbs, Morgan and Taylor, 1984; Holly and Morgan, 1993) have explored students' views on how they come to be studying, by using individual in-depth interviews. Students were asked, 'How did you come to be studying with the university?' and 'How did you come to be taking this course?' Similar research has also been carried out among engineering technicians studying an open learning course, produced by the Open Tech in the UK (Strang, 1987).

Although the main focus of this book is on open and distance learning, where students are very often studying on a part-time basis, research carried out with students engaged in full-time study at conventional universities is also relevant. This point is particularly pertinent at a time when conventional universities are increasingly beginning to adopt self-study or distance learning materials as part of their teaching and learning provision, and also when the boundaries between different sectors in post-compulsory education are rapidly becoming blurred.

Here are six students explaining how they came to be studying the Social Science Foundation Course at the Open University (Taylor, Morgan and Gibbs, 1981). (None of the students in the sample in this study had the formal qualifications usually required for university entrance.)

I suppose I want to prove something to myself. The one piece [on the OU] I have read said it was the most difficult way anybody had yet devised to get a degree and I thought – if I can do it at least it will prove something to me if nobody else and I'd like to do that.

I suppose it was waking up one morning and finding that I'm 35 – a sort of male menopause – can't sit around here watching television for the rest of my life – let's do something now.

I have got nothing behind me, absolutely nothing – no qualifications. I've only had odd jobs before and as soon as she (young daughter) is old enough I'll have to get a job. Somebody said to me, 'The OU is your best bet'. It's an educational basis, something behind me. If I went for a job now, I wouldn't have a chance, no way. I know nothing except factory work and that's not what I want. I am not that bright, but I am not thick either, you know. So I want something so I can go and get a decent job.

It's relevant to my work, it [social sciences] appealed to me because the reaction of people is terribly important in my work in personnel. I want to know the reason people react under various kinds of circumstances. The course is important because I hope it will help me to understand people more. But I'm not going to use my qualification at the end of the day, so that side is not important to me.

I wanted to do something as a next step. I've done evening classes, but it wasn't enough really – I've got through that sort of stage.

Its purely interest in the subject, because if it was for a career I'd be doing a science course, it's the subject first. I'm interested in sociology which I've done a bit before and I learnt a lot about the way society works, but in itself it is not enough to explain a lot of things. I know very little about political science, I want to know more about that. Economics is something of closed book to me at present, yet it obviously plays a very important part in the way our society works. Understanding, you could sum it up like that for me.

So we have quite a diverse range of explanations for registering on an OU course. Let's try to unpack what lies behind these different descriptions.

The first student refers to proving to herself that she is capable of university level study. For the second student, he seems concerned to do something different in an attempt to change or broaden his life and hopes that part-time university study will enable this to occur. The third quotation indicates clearly the vocational focus of this student's concerns, that is to gain some form of qualification to enable her to get a job other than relatively unskilled factory work. The fourth student has vocational concerns, but these are very different from the previous student. He works as a personnel officer and wants the content of the course to help him perform better at his job. The fifth student has already been doing evening classes and sees part-time study at university level as the next step up the educational ladder. The final quotation shows a student who has an intrinsic interest in the subject of understanding society.

These students are not more motivated or less in their studies – on the contrary. They have very different aims and purposes in registering for a foundation course with the Open University. To understand the variations in aims and purposes among students is not merely an academic research exercise. This understanding helps us to make sense of how students are tackling particular learning activities in a course. Orientation to education is defined as 'all those attitudes, aims and purposes which express a student's relationship with a course and with the university' (Taylor, Morgan and Gibbs, 1981). From the six students quoted above, the three main orientations of personal, vocational and academic can be identified. (These are explained in detail later in this chapter.) In terms of evaluating a course, so as to improve students' learning, the concept of orientation to education forms the crucial basis of a student's relationship to a course. It forms the broad 'backcloth' for understanding how and why students tackle their work in particular ways. It relates a student's social and domestic contexts into the more detailed issues of studying a particular course.

Perhaps you are thinking that the diversity of students' orientations identified among OU students is peculiar to that institution, with its mature student population and its open entry policy. This is not the case. Studies of students in conventional full-time education, where the student population might be expected to be more homogeneous, also show a considerable diversity. The following quotations are from interviews with students who were doing a degree in Human Sciences at Surrey University (Taylor, 1983).

It was interest really. At school I had done a science course and I didn't particularly like it. So I went back after I'd worked for a year and did sociology, which I liked. I didn't just want to do sociology, I wanted to do philosophy as well – so I applied out of my interest in sociology, because I wanted to do that anyway.

I always wanted to go to University, but I was prevented from doing so by the Second World War and I've only now had the chance to come to university. I see university as an enrichment of life. My main interest is with philosophy and this course is one that deals with it and also uses philosophy so I applied for it.

I wanted to go into educational counselling and I knew it would be difficult to get on a course even with teaching experience because it's very selective. So I thought I'd try and get a degree at Surrey and then go on into educational psychology. It's really with a view to getting a job. I want a job that's connected with mental health and vocational guidance.

I was at direct grant school and it was very geared to education. To go to university was just the accepted thing, everybody went to university. And my father and mother went to university. As far as my choice of courses was concerned, it was based on 'what am I going to be willing to spend three years of my life doing?'

To have a good time is part of it for me. I mean what is education? It's just as valid to go and talk to someone in a pub or to read a book. I don't think it is more important, you know, to read a book than to meet people.

Again, quite a wide range of explanations and expectations here for taking a course, although it was a multi-disciplinary course comprising sociology, philosophy and psychology. A diverse range of student interests like this can serve as a salutary reminder to academic staff, who sometimes believe that the students' sole purpose is the same as their own, namely the pursuit of academic scholarship in its own right.

How can we interpret these quotations from conventional university students? How do they compare with the group of OU students? The first student is clearly interested in the subject, particularly sociology and philosophy and is looking for a place where he can continue to study in the same areas. The second quotation shows a student who wants to engage in higher education as a way to enrich his life. The third student seems to have quite a well thought out career path. She sees the course as a means to an end to gain the necessary qualifications for entry to a specialism. The last two students seem to be different. Any specific interest in the course is barely discernible. The fourth student feels pushed into university by parental pressure and pressure from school; in terms of course choice, he is merely trying to find something to do for three years, given the inevitability of his move from school to university. The final student is expressing a strong interest in the social dimension to education. He also expresses a belief in less formal learning methods, namely, talking with people in the pub!

Again, these students are not more, or less, motivated to their studies (although some of the more traditional academic staff might shudder to hear some of these reasons). They have very different aims and purposes for engaging in university education. Or to put it more formally, they have very different orientations to education.

For school leavers to gain a place at university the competition is considerable, in spite of more recent efforts to increase participation levels. Even though there is much pressure towards vocational aspects of the university experience and the training of a skilled workforce, there are still wide variations between students of the sort described above. As teachers and course designers in education and training, we need to know more about the aims and aspirations of our students if we are to take improving the quality of our teaching and learning provisions at all seriously. Orientation to education provides a concept which can be regarded as a 'holistic' motivation, as viewed from the student's perspective. The variations between these orientations can be described under three main headings of Personal, Vocational and Academic Orientations, each divided into extrinsic and intrinsic orientations and also a Social Orientation (with the full-time conventional university students). Although the quotations here are from students in higher education, the concept of orientation to education is widely applicable in education and training. For example, Sagar and Strang (1985) have used orientation to understand variations between engineering technician students following an Open Tech open learning course.

The variations between orientations are summarized in Table 1. In the next section each of these orientations will be looked at in turn.

Orientations to education

Personal intrinsic orientation

This category is characterized by students who are personally orientated and are concerned with the 'broadening' aspects of university education and see it as a means of changing. This personal orientation is particularly common with OU students as they commence their first foundation course. For some students engaging in open learning with OU, there is a feeling of frustration with their lives. (Quotations from student interviews are taken from Taylor, Gibbs and Morgan, 1980, unless otherwise stated. Some of them were also quoted in Gibbs, Morgan and Taylor, 1984.)

Orientation	Interest	Aim	Concerns
Vocational	Intrinsic	Training	Relevance of course to future career
	Extrinsic	Qualification	Recognition of worth of qualification
Academic	Intrinsic	Following intellectual interest	Room to choose stimulating lectures
	Extrinsic	Educational progression	Grades, academic progress
Personal	Intrinsic	Broadening or Self-improvement	Challenge, interesting material.
	Extrinsic	Compensation or Proof of capability	Passing course, feedback
Social	Extrinsic	Having a good time	Facilities for sport and social activities

Table 1 *Students' educational orientations* (Gibbs, Morgan and Taylor, 1984, p 170)

> I hadn't thought about it [OU study] at all but I had to do something. I thought I was going round the bend being at home and I wasn't raring to go to get a job. I like looking after the house and the baby and that sort of thing, but somehow I wanted to do something else.

The importance of the course to students like this one is how it can change them as individuals and broaden their perspectives on life. They see their study as primarily of personal significance.

> It is important to *me* because it's the only thing that is me and that only I'm doing and that none of my family or friends are doing. It doesn't matter to anyone else results wise how you get on – and I think it is purely you doing it and you getting something out of it for yourself.

The actual choice of course is almost irrelevant and was likely to have been made by a process of elimination of the alternatives, rather than by a specific choice of subject area. These students hoped that the course (the social science foundation course in this study) would help their understanding of everyday life. These students' aims about broadening are clearly evident from their responses to questions about expectations of the course and what they hoped to gain from it.

> Well I expect to get a better insight into the way other people think. I think one tends to be very biased – you live your own life and that is the way it is. I'm hoping that I'll be able to see things from different points of view and not be too single-minded about things. I hope at the end I'll be able to converse with people more easily without getting nervous.

Personal extrinsic orientation

In contrast to students with a personal broadening orientation (above), those with personal extrinsic orientations are taking a course to prove their abilities to themselves and their friends. Many of these students feel they have been unfairly judged by the educational system in the past, and regard part-time study with the OU as a way of 'compensation' to test and to prove their abilities. These students tend to be very concerned with grades and feedback. This type of orientation is common in the OU. Again it can be seen as a form of compensation for the lack of higher education in the past. For many of these students the opportunities through open and distance learning are the only ones available to them, both because of time factors and also access, due to their relative lack of formal entry qualifications for university level study. These students are concerned to find out whether they are up to university level study.

> Basically, I just want to see if I can do it. I'm not aiming for a degree at the end, that would be a bonus at the end of however many years. If I only get half way through the foundation course and discover, yes it is too much for me, for my brain and my time, that's fair enough. I've proved the point to myself and that's where I shall stop I guess.

Students whose orientation is towards compensation, are often studying with a feeling of competition with others. There is a feeling that if friends or neighbours are capable of OU study, then they must be as well. For these students, almost as soon as they start the course there is concern to 'stay the course' and to see it through to the end. For example:

> It [OU course] is very important, now I have started it . . . I feel that I've probably not had a challenge [before] . . . to have to do some-thing so important for myself, so I have to prove it, perhaps to myself that I can stick with it . . . I feel it's going to be the only chance I have got and if I drop out I won't get another chance in the foreseeable future.

There are parallels between these studies, which have developed 'orientation to education' as an analytical concept, and early studies in the OU carried out for the OU by an external market research bureau. Goodyear (1975) conducted group discussions with students from a number of courses and at various stages towards their degrees to investigate their attitudes and reasons for studying. This study used an interesting distinction of 'qualification' and 'compensation' as two key contrasting reasons for registering for an OU degree. Qualification is where the reason is: 'Obtaining a specific qualification in order to achieve some promotion at work', whereas compensation is where students are 'searching for something to compensate inadequacies in one's existing life'.

Students whose aim is qualification want a degree in order to improve their job opportunities. They have usually had some contact with the academic world. In contrast, students whose reasons are concerned with compensation have felt cheated out of educational experiences due to inaccurate assessment of their ability, and they feel they are not valued in the world in the way they deserve. These distinctions of qualification and compensation can be related closely to the categories of vocational and personal orientations. Compensation is linked to particular anxiety about studying and fear of failure.

> At the moment I intend to pass, I don't think I could live with myself if I failed. If I fail I'm going to be absolutely shattered – so I've got to pass. (Student quoted in Goodyear, 1975)

Goodyear also suggested that this kind of very anxious student who worries about possible problems is likely to have 'an inefficiently high drive, which could cause complete breakdown and subsequent drop-out'.

An understanding of students' orientations to education is particularly important as it links together the details of how students tackle a course or a particular assignment and broader issues of their social and domestic contexts of study. To understand the extrinsic nature of some students' orientations to education, reminds us of the major emotional issues which are so often intimately connected with how a student comes to be studying. Orientation to education is a crucial concept for helping to understand the counselling perspective for students. It is as relevant for full-time students in conventional universities as it is for those studying part-time in open and distance learning.

Vocational extrinsic orientation

In the case of this vocational orientation, the emphasis is on the qualification aspects of the course or degree profile. Students are concerned about *qualification*, as it is seen as a means to an end to get a job. For many OU students, they have no particular job in mind, but hope in an unspecified way that getting a degree will help them in the future. Many of these students are women planning to return to work after having spent a number of years bringing up children.

> When the OU was first set up I thought that when the time came that would be for me. At that time I had one baby. I thought that when they were all at school, I would do it. Partly because I don't want to go back to purely secretarial work, I'd rather do something different, and I don't want to do a job that will interfere with the children, so it [OU course] seemed a useful way to occupy my time.

For other students, there is some concern that their employers would recognize an OU degree, as they need the qualification to enhance their promotion prospects.

> To get into the top of this hierarchy is going to be quite hard . . . I've got two sets of professional qualifications but I need a degree. Because in a lot of people's eyes, particularly management trainers, a degree is everything. It proves you've done something, it proves you've trained yourself to think and express yourself clearly.

For some conventional university full-time students, a vocational extrinsic orientation leads them do the minimum to pass in order to get a degree. Some students have investigated how far the actual grade of degree mattered in gaining a job and on that basis decided how much work to put into their studies. Some students decide that grades are not particularly important. So, we can understand how these students come to be doing little beyond the minimum requirements of the assessment system, given their aims to get a pass degree.

Vocational intrinsic orientation

A vocational intrinsic orientation describes students who are following a course where its content is relevant to training for a particular job or for a future career. In the research at Surrey University (Taylor, 1983), one of the studies was with students doing a degree in Hotel and Catering Administration. Many of these students were vocationally orientated, but there was a significant difference in students' concerns depending on whether their aims were to get a qualification, as an entry into the industry, or to be trained as hotel managers. The second group was interested in the course content, and was critical of parts they thought were not relevant to their future careers. These students placed considerable emphasis on the practical side of the course and particularly valued the industrial placement.

With OU students, they are concerned about the course content in relation to their current employment. For example a student doing an OU computing course (Morgan, 1988):

> I wanted to know more about computers, background knowledge to help me understand more about the system we use in here at work.

This vocational orientation is characterized by an intrinsic interest in the course content and how this is likely to help students in their work. The distinction between vocational intrinsic and vocational extrinsic orientations was found by Sagar and Strang (1985) to be particularly important for understanding how Open Tech engineering technicians went about their studies.

Academic intrinsic orientation

This category of orientation is characterized by students who have a strong interest in the particular subject – an intellectual interest to study the subject for its own sake. For example, an OU student doing a computing course, although well qualified in different areas (Morgan, 1988):

> I'm interested in the course to be more in control of computers through understanding more about them. It is not going to affect my work, I've got enough consultancy to keep me going for the rest of my life. It is a personal interest in computers and eventually to get an OU degree with a computing profile, but more degrees is the last thing I need really.

Students with this type of orientation often want to pursue their own intellectual interests, even though this can be at odds with the formal course requirements, as the following student explained:

> I wanted to do sociology, the interesting thing about sociology is that in the sociology of education, in studying education I've become more aware of it in an objective way, you start to see its place in society. Sociology isn't a nine to five study, it's a continual thing in your social life, you are being a sociologist. You are assessed . . . so you've got to do a certain amount of course . . . I try to do the minimum amount of work in psychology and philosophy, but in sociology I just try to do as much reading as I can and when I write essays I always bring in much more. I hardly ever answer the question, I'm always much too concerned with other things of interest to *me*.' (Taylor, 1983)

Although the student quoted above is perhaps pursuing his own interests to an extreme – the desire to be 'syllabus-free' at the expense of the formal course requirements – the intrinsic interest in the subject is the crucial aspect of this orientation.

Academic extrinsic orientation

This type of orientation describes students who are pursuing the next step on the educational ladder. In the OU this may be students who are progressing from evening classes. With little formal educational background, these students, having 'made a start' with some form of evening class or preparatory course, are now registering for an OU foundation course. This orientation is much more prevalent with full-time students in conventional universities. Getting to university has almost 'happened to them', as the expected progression from school. In the fictional autobiography in Chapter 1 we saw how the student almost 'drifted' into university, following the best subject from A-level studies, as the next step on the educational ladder.

Students who are orientated in this way tend to be concerned with success in the course and tend to be 'syllabus-bound', they are mainly concerned with getting good grades as part of the academic 'game'. Although they are following a subject because they were good at it at school, they are more interested in getting the grades than with scholarship and learning for its own sake, hence the notion that study is 'extrinsic' to the student.

Social orientation

A social orientation is characterized by students whose main interests lie with the social opportunities of university life, rather than those directly connected with a particular course. Clearly this is likely to apply mainly to conventional students studying full-time. For example:

> The outside activities that I do in the radio and film unit and sport are very important. There is a lot to do outside and in some respects I tend to put off work because of them. From the point of view of a university education, this side of it is just as important as the academic side, if not more important. I suppose you can always study by correspondence, but you can't get this kind of social thing and development anywhere else. (Taylor, 1983)

Social orientation seems to be extrinsic to a course of study, but students will often describe aspects of academic and vocational orientations as well.

For mature students studying part-time by open or distance learning, this is clearly quite different. However, some of the learning activities do have a directly social or group dimension to them. For example, in the OU, the tutorial provision at a local level provides a unique social opportunity for a group of students who often have very diverse backgrounds. For some of these students, support available from their peers can be vitally important to them, when little or sometimes no support is offered in their domestic contexts. Also in the OU, residential schools have a directly social dimension. Some students tend to choose courses which have residential requirements, because they value and enjoy the more informal aspects of learning in a group setting and the social contact available to them.

So these descriptions of orientation provide the 'flesh' on the summary set out in Table 1, above. However, it is important to realize that these are 'idealized' descriptions of students. They provide an analytical framework for interpreting how students describe how they come to be engaged in study. In reality, of course, students are more complex. Any particular student will often be quite a complex combination of two or more of these ideal orientations.

Many OU students can be seen to have a mixture of orientations. For example:

> I hope to stop myself from turning into a complete cabbage and to widen my views on life. Eventually I hope to get a degree and possibly that will help me to get a job, one which I would like to do. But I think that is very much a secondary consideration at the moment.

There is clearly a personal broadening orientation here, linked to a secondary vocational one. Both these orientations will influence how the student approaches studying. Also it is likely that the relative importance of the two will change during the student's career as she gains course credits and progresses towards a degree.

Using orientation: evaluating home computing

Orientation to education is central to understanding students' experiences of study, as it enables us, as teachers, trainers and course designers, to make the link between a student's social, political and domestic context on one hand, and the more detailed issues about how they actually tackle learning activities in a specific course, on the other. Putting orientation into action generates insights which are vital for course evaluation. Without detailed knowledge of students' aims and purposes we are not in a position to interpret and analyse what students are saying about a particular course or part of a course. Students' study patterns are influenced by what they want to gain from a course.

This section will look at how orientation has been used in course evaluation with part-time distance education students in the OU. The first example (Morgan, 1988) is part of an evaluation of students studying a second-level course in computing, entitled, 'The Fundamentals of Computing' (OU course code M205).

In this study a group of sixteen students were asked in individual face-to-face interviews how they came be taking the course and what they hoped to gain from it. Although there can be no claims for statistical generalizability in small-scale studies, this study was carried out by adopting the strategy of 'theoretical sampling'. In this approach, data collection and analysis proceed concurrently. New interview subjects are selected according to their potential for refining and developing the emerging themes and concepts. In this study, students were selected from the OU Welsh Region, as this area seemed a likely place to be able to sample what could be loosely termed 'remote students'. This sample was selected in an attempt to include the key issues of educational background, sex, class, occupation and experience of study with the OU.

The concept of orientation was used to interpret how students came to be engaged in study. Also, over a number of years of part-time study there were important changes in orientation. The notion of *change* is particularly important for mature adults studying part-time at a distance. There are two major dimensions to change: change in students' lives, in personal and domestic terms; and also change in career terms. There is a continuous interaction or dialectic between these aspects of students' lives and these have a crucial impact on students' choices and decisions and on how and why they study. This analysis provides holistic understanding of students. It puts 'life' into educational evaluation in distance education. (There are parallels here with the work of Goodson and Walker (1988), in school-based evaluations.) Although there are many differences between students, it is possible to represent them by means of a small number of major variations or distinct 'types'. This study developed a typology describing five major variations as follows: (i) professionals using computers in their work; (ii) students wanting a degree for a job change; (iii) women returning to work; (iv) students with a general interest in computers; and (v) computer professionals. By developing a typology of this nature, more general statements about the students can be made at the same time as maintaining holistic descriptions of individual students. This typology will now be outlined briefly to demonstrate how this builds on the concept of orientation to education.

Professionals using computers

There was a distinctive group of students, engaged in a range of professions, including geological research consultancy, production management, and water resource management, who all used computers in some way in their work. For these students one of their aims in studying the course was 'to get to know more about computers'. The OU computing course would help them with their work, but only in a fairly general way. Maths and computing were also personal interests which had developed from the content of their work. These students were in senior positions in their work careers, and although their formal educational qualifications were at Higher National Diploma (HND) or Higher National Certificate (HNC), their work experience was now more important in career terms than getting a degree. They had considerable background knowledge of computers, but were not necessarily experienced in PASCAL programming, which is central to the course. As one student working in the water industry explained:

> I use a bit of maths in our work on sludge treatment and I got interested in maths . . . It was a personal interest initially, so I decided to do it properly and I took the Maths Foundation Course. I probably won't use it really, but we do some maths in the work in water treatment. We work with engineers on site meetings, so it is nice to know more of what is involved, rather than just taking what they say as experts.

Another student had applied computers to cartography in an innovative way and had gained promotion in his organization to head of department; in career terms he was clearly very successful. But it was personal interest which attracted him to OU study:

> I wanted some mental stimulation. I've got a son at university and a colleague in the finance department here has just got an OU maths degree and I have friends doing OU study, so I put in to the company [to get the course fees] to do a degree. I did the Technology Foundation Course and thoroughly enjoyed it. It was really stimulating, although towards the end it was a bit of a struggle.

Further on in the interview he explained how he was finding the course:

> I wanted to know more about computers, background knowledge to help me understand more about the system here [in his workplace], rather than the details of programming. I've got PASCAL programmers working for me upstairs!

In relation to orientation to education, these students can be understood in terms of a combination of academic and vocational intrinsic orientations. It is this intrinsic nature of these orientations which is the key feature of this 'idealized type' of student. Although they are professionals using computers and want to improve their understanding of them, OU study seems unlikely to be very important to them in terms of career progression.

Students wanting a job change

There was another clearly identifiable group of students who wanted an OU degree to help them with a change of job or a specific career promotion. These students all had some background in post-compulsory education, up to HND level. The key feature of these students was that their prime reason for OU study was to get a qualification in order to change jobs.

For example, one student who had left school, then gone to technical college, was working as a panel beater. He was in his late twenties and appeared to be comfortable in the material sense, but he wanted to get a degree as quickly as possible and was aiming to take one-and-a-half credits per year (6 credits are required for a degree).

> I am trying to change jobs and I want a degree . . . I want a computer oriented job. I've looked at things in administration, but they are poorly paid . . . working with my hands pays better at the moment . . . Daddy was right, I should have stayed on at school, gone to college and got some qualifications.

In terms of orientation to education, a vocational extrinsic orientation would describe this student. In a similar example, a student in his early twenties, working as a marine engineer, doing M205 as his second course after the maths foundation course explained:

> I've always wanted to get a degree, but wanted some cash, so I left school after A-level and did an apprenticeship and an OND (Ordinary National Diploma) and an HND in marine engineering by part-time study. As a marine engineer you're a jack of all trades, practical engi-

neering knowledge, computer work and control etc. I wanted a degree and was interested in computers at school . . . I'd played around in BASIC but I thought it was time I learnt about it properly . . . so I'm doing M205.'

His work schedules, which involved long periods at sea, made keeping up with the course quite difficult. He was very short of time for study and spent most of his leave studying. In spite of these problems he was determined to succeed:

I'll get there in the end. I've done two years now and I won't give up. On leave, my life is studying for a degree, compared to friends who just seem to waste time . . . I'll get the Ordinary Degree and then I'll get a better paid job sorted out.

Within this group, two students had gained the promotion they wanted before graduation and this had a considerable influence on their studies. The very strong desire to get a degree as a route to a better job sometimes changed quite dramatically. For example, one student had left school, then done an HNC in production engineering, but he wanted a degree for a change of job.

I want to get a degree whilst working, there's not much cash in repairing aircraft, so I started on T101 then did M101 and now M205 this year. I've just got a new job as a technical sales executive, so a degree is less important now.

He commented how the pay in his new job was very good and that any further job change might be towards technical sales, as he gained more knowledge about computers from OU study. It seemed clear that he had already succeeded in changing jobs before completing his undergraduate studies.

The phenomenon of job change and promotion during study sometimes resulted in dropout, as a production manager in his forties explained:

I've always wanted to go to university and get a degree, but I left school, did an HNC part-time. I've done T101, TM222 [The Digital Computer] and TM281 [Modelling with Mathematics] – but some of the rush has gone out of it now. I've been promoted. It's experience that counts now . . . I was doing an assignment one weekend recently, the family was around the house and I just thought 'What am I doing?' My priorities have changed really, I'm about to drop out now . . . perhaps I'll come back to it later when the children are older.

These two examples can be seen as the paradigm case of *change* in orientation to study. There were other less 'extreme' cases of change; for example, teachers moving from physical sciences into computing in response to job vacancies and chances of promotion, and also students taking early retirement, but aiming to add computing knowledge to their existing expertise, in order to give them a chance of a 'second career', or some part-time work in the future.

The importance of change in career is that it can have a crucial impact on how a student tackles the course. That is the interaction between the 'lines' of career as a student and career in terms of employment. This overall social context of study is important to understand when interpreting how and why students tackle their work.

Women returning to work

Women returning to work, or planning to in the near future, also seem to form a distinctive group. The style of part-time study with learning materials based primarily on individual home-based study suits these students, as a student in her early twenties with a young baby explained:

> I'm not wanting a career in computing at the moment, that's in the future, I just love computing! . . . I always liked the logic of working things out, that's the main beauty of it all. It's brilliant to have the computer all the time, it's really marvellous to get all the education I want, it really suits me.

In terms of orientation, vocational and academic intrinsic orientations describe this student.

Another student in this study was taking the course in order to update her qualifications and compete in the job market.

> I worked in computers for ICL eight years ago, before I had children. I was working part time until last year . . . I needed to prove I was up to date in computers, especially as I have no formal qualification in computing, so I started with the OU on M101 . . . It was the only thing [part-time higher education] around here. I've got a full-time job now so it's a bit different . . . but I still want the qualification, although I have much less time to study now.

Although there are similarities between this student and the previous group (a vocational extrinsic orientation), the nature of the course, with a home computer, raises gender issues which are specific to women's experiences.

In contrast to using computers in the more competitive male-dominated atmosphere of local tutorials or residential school, the home computer can be particularly valuable for women students, assuming they have good access to the computer in their own domestic environment.

Students with a general interest in computers

Another group of students described their interest in computers in very general terms, for example, 'computers are going to be very important in work in the future' or 'it's about time I knew more about computers'. In terms of orientation to study, it could be regarded as academic and/or vocational. However, a key feature of these students was the vagueness of their interest in computing, and also they were all novices at programming. They were struggling with the course and appeared to be on the point of dropping out when they were interviewed half way through it. For example, a student in his twenties working in a local factory said:

> I thought M205 would be interesting and about computers. I've messed about in BASIC . . . I've got a sort of hobbyist interest in computers. I've found the course very difficult . . . I've been working weekends and have not had much time for it, I've missed the last two TMAs, so I'll probably drop out.

Although he put his difficulties down to a lack of time, he appeared to lack a clear focus in his OU study other than a vague hobby interest in computers.

Other students who wanted to gain a broad general knowledge of computers were surprised at the large amount of programming required. It appeared that their interest in the course was not sufficient to sustain them 'to stick at' the programming which was needed to complete the assignments. This is quite a major task for students new to programming and drop-out from the course seemed likely for them.

Computer experts

There also seemed to be a distinctive group of computer experts – they use computers regularly and are also experienced programmers. For example, one student described himself as an academic who had moved into computing. He was working as a self-employed consultant using computers in linguistics (see second quotation on p 37).

This interest in the course is not so different from that of other students, a vocational and personal intrinsic orientation. However, because of the nature of the student's work and his computing experience, his response to the course was very different. He was much more critical in terms of content and pedagogy of the course, particularly the home computing activities.

Orientation in course evaluation

The above typology was developed as part of a course evaluation project by using the concept of orientation to education to interpret student interviews. Some groups of students are not represented directly in this typology, however, for example the unemployed and students from ethnic minorities. Also, it is not the only typology which could have been developed. However, this framework represents a 'recognizable reality' for understanding students. When we are aware of the variations in students' experiences, as teachers, trainers and course designers in open and distance learning we shall be in a better position to understand how and why students tackle their studies.

This understanding does not generate neat prescriptions for improving learning. Rather it provides a major input to our 'reflection-in-action' (Schon, 1983) on student learning. Holistic descriptions of students give insights into the details of students' study processes and the problems they encounter. This understanding serves to raise our awareness about studying, as viewed from the student perspective. Schon (1983) makes the distinction between 'technical rationality' and 'reflection-in-action' to describe how professionals operate, and how they come to change or modify their practice. We can see a close parallel in open and distance learning regarding course evaluation. Much of the literature on course development, evaluation and course improvement in open and distance learning describes a rational systems approach (see for example Rowntree, 1982, 1985). This approach is a valuable starting point: it is the technical rationality in Schon's terminology. However, it does not provide a fully adequate understanding of the course-development process. The rational systems approach is a necessary part of course development and evaluation in open and distance learning, but other factors, namely the micro-politics, sub-cultures and history of the organization, also have a vital influence (Altrichter, Evans, and Morgan, 1991).

An understanding of students' orientations to education provides an essential dimension to 'reflection-in-action' for course designers to reflect critically on their practice, as part of the process of improving student learning. It is a concept which can be used in a variety of educational settings and levels. So for example, Holt, Petzall and Viljoen (1990) have used orientation to help them understand more about how a group of students came to be studying for a Master in Business Administration by part-time external study at an Australian university.

In distance education and open learning, where there is usually a physical separation of teacher and learner, finding out about students' responses to a course is a key aspect of 'teaching' a course. Postal survey methods are often used to elicit students' responses to teaching materials, by means of rating scales on 'helpfulness', 'interest' and 'difficulty', for example. This sort of routine monitoring can be seen as a form of quality control in distance education: it gives a 'broad brush' glimpse at quality. However, this type of research and evaluation makes data interpretation problematic, as it takes no account of the subjectivity in students' aims and purposes for studying. Orientation to education provides a conceptual framework for understanding the learners' realities of studying.

Orientation and students' study patterns

So far we have seen some of the diversity of how students come to be engaged in study, and that orientation to education can be regarded as an 'holistic motivation', which forms the background to how students tackle particular learning tasks, especially to how they relate to the assessment system. Students with different orientations will direct their attentions to quite different aspects of the course. This can be highlighted by quotations from two students doing a course in Hotel and Catering Administration (Taylor, 1983).

> The thing I've been a bit shocked about is that we only spend a single afternoon in the kitchens . . . I feel it ought to be at least two afternoons a week to start to be any use. It's a case of playtime really . . . just a case of 'oh well, we've only got a single afternoon in the kitchen, what should we do to fill the time' . . . it's a waste of time really.

> I suppose it's a lot more practical than I expected. We spend a lot of time in the kitchens and it's not academic enough. I thought it would be more academic being at a university . . . but this course is not in my view.

The first student sees the course as a training and wants the course to be more practical than it is, whereas the second student is concerned with academic progression and she considers the course to be too practical. Clearly neither view is right or wrong; the course actually falls short of both their expectations and consequently fails to please either of them.

Students have different reasons for taking a course and engaging in education and training, and the differences in their orientations lead to different concerns and likes and dislikes in the teaching. As students are attempting to gain different things from study, this has a direct influence on their study patterns. It would seem likely that students who need very good degrees to be sure of getting the jobs they want, will be more concerned about assessment than those whose main purpose in coming to university is to have a good time socially. It can also be seen that students who are mainly concerned in gaining a qualification differ in terms of level of qualification they need. One of the students quoted in the introduction to this Chapter was concerned to get an upper second class degree to be sure of getting a place on a professional training course. She planned her work very carefully, kept well up to date with the assessed course work and was getting high grades. Contrast this study pattern with the following student:

> Most of the work I do is just to get the marks and that's it. It shouldn't be like this at university but it is for me. I'm in for a third [class degree] at the moment, I think I'm better than a third, but I'm not that bothered because I don't think our degree is recognized that much by industry, and and you could say that it's not that important. As long as I get a pass mark . . . then good. I'm not the sort of person to go all out to do the best I can, I just go out to get a reasonable mark. (Taylor, 1983)

Both students want to gain a qualification for a particular job, but whereas for the first student a good grade is necessary, the second feels it is not worth the effort and only a pass grade is needed. So we see that how these students tackle their work is closely geared to the assessment system and the qualification they are aiming for. The main point is that the amount of effort students put in to studying, and how that effort is directed, is logical in relation to their individual aims and purposes in being in higher education.

To summarize, students' orientations and how they respond to the assessment demands made of them have a crucial impact on how they actually go about their studies. In Chapter 4, we shall look in detail at the variations in students' approaches to learning and how these are intimately bound up with the nature of the assessment system. By developing our understanding of these issues from the student's perspective, we shall be in a better position to reflect upon and theorize our teaching and learning practice, as the basis for improving student learning.

Finally, you may like to pause and consider the following questions:

- How does orientation to education relate to the students you are teaching or training?
- What are your implicit assumptions about your learners – are they really quite the homogeneous group of learners you may think they are?
- Do your learners have the same sorts of interests about the education and training you are providing as you do?
- To what extent is there mismatch between the aims of your courses and the likely aims and aspirations of your students?

You may like to ask your learners how they came to be following your course, as part of a formative evaluation activity. With the data you collect, are you able to construct a typology (as above) of your learners' aims and aspirations?

Chapter 3
What is learning?

In this Chapter I want to extend the discussion of students' experiences of learning to look at what students believe learning itself consists of. This is not merely an academic exercise. Across all sectors of education and training, the way in which students perceive learning influences how they tackle their learning activities. Also for teachers, trainers and course designers, if we are to make progress with improving our students' learning, we need to be clearer about the sorts of understanding, knowledge and skills we want to develop with our students. This is not a call for the return to behavioural objectives and the views of learning embodied in much of instructional technology, which has been heavily influenced by behavioural psychology. On the contrary, I am suggesting that we need to 'theorize our practice', to ask critical questions about the content and pedagogy of our educational practices. And at the same time we need to become more aware of the ways in which students are grappling with their own study processes as they engage with our courses.

Learning and the aims of education and training

What is learning? Why is it important to address this question? Although I have used 'improving your students' learning' in the title of this book, I have not discussed 'learning' in any detail so far. In some respects, learning is such a pervasive term that its meaning is taken for granted. So in the universities, historically the centres of academia, learning has been associated with knowledge and understanding, with using concepts, critical reading of the literature, developing theories, and scholarship and research. There is little doubt that these issues are central to the mission of the universities, polytechnics, and institutes of higher education throughout the world.

However, as we are concerned here with improving learning, we need a much more detailed analysis of what we mean by learning, particularly as we are looking at it in rather different settings from that of the conventional university. Open and distance learning is central to education and training in a wide range of sectors, from purpose-designed distance teaching universities, such as the OU in the UK and Athabasca University in Canada, to external study in the 'dual-mode' Australian universities (with both on-campus and off-campus students), to vocationally focused education and training courses, including management education, nurse education, health and safety in the catering industry, etc, etc. In some respects the newness of open and distance learning has demanded a degree of 'theorizing' about learning, as there are not the established institutions with long histories and traditions. Thus considerable attention has been given to questions about 'what to teach, how to teach it and how to assess it'. Teachers, trainers and academics, often with the assistance of educational technologists and course designers, have been engaged in fundamental debates about the aims and purposes of their courses.

At the same time as the growth of open and distance learning, there has been considerable pressure in the UK from the Conservative Government to reform higher education and make it more responsive to the needs of industry. The vocational training sector in the UK, encouraged by the former Man-power Services Commission and then the Training Agency, has embraced 'open learning' almost as the new panacea for all training and education problems. Also in the UK, the Enterprise in Higher Education (EHE) initiative promoted by the Training Agency (now by the Department of Employment) set out to reform curriculum and teaching methods in higher education and to introduce 'enterprise' into the curriculum. The EHE projects currently in operation are likely to have a continuing influence on the debates about the curriculum in higher education. In the vocational sector, the National Council for Vocational Qualifications is developing a series of levels of National Vocational Qualifications (NVQs) related to competency-based training and education. These qualifications will span a wide range of educational levels. In fact, NVQ Level 5 is proposed to be equivalent to degree level, hence the great importance of vocational issues for the universities. Irrespective of the nature of the political agendas driving some of these changes, competencies and skills are now entering the vocabulary of the debates about education at all levels. If we ignore the implications of these changes, we are likely to be left 'struggling against the tide' of the current debates in education and training.

Changes in the student population require us to ask fundamental ques-tions about education and training. With the increasing number of mature students entering conventional universities and polytechnics, for both full-time and part-time study, there are various initiatives to recognize learning gained outside formal education and from the experience of work by the 'accreditation of prior learning'. With the abolition in 1992 of the binary divide in the UK between universities and polytechnics, there is now a rapid increase in credit transfer between different institutions. Also access initiatives to increase student participation in higher education require careful analysis of learning and teaching. With these changes, students' learning experiences, in terms of knowledge and skills, are a vital part of the discussions. So, if the language for debates about education and training is changing, how is 'learning' referred to? How are knowledge and understanding described in relation to education and training of skills and competencies?

Although much of the literature on competency is concerned with how to recognize it and how to assess it, there is concern that competency assessment should not be narrowly focused on observable aspects of performance in the workplace. Some of the recent statements about assessment of competence also refer to knowledge and understanding, as well as performance. For example, the 'Code of Practice' set out by the Training Agency states that:

> Each element of competence should describe something that a person who works in a particular occupational area should be able to do: an action, behaviour or outcome which the person should be able to demonstrate. Or it should describe a knowledge or understanding which is essential in that it underpins sustained performance or facilitates the extension of skill to new situations within the occupation. (Black and Wolf, 1990, p 6)

This statement is open to a variety of interpretations. At one level, it could be seen as the re-emergence of behavioural approaches to learning under the guise of skill and competence – behavioural objectives again 'by the back door'. Although the extravagant claims of the 'behaviour objectives movement' in the 1960s and 1970s have not been achieved in practice, they did provide an impetus for the scrutiny of much education and training. For the 'champions' of workplace assessment, this statement from the Training Agency could be seen as a step back from focusing on competence in the workplace, by making reference to assessing more conventional academic knowledge and understanding. Michael Eraut has made an important contribution to this debate, by stressing the crucial importance of basic underlying knowledge associated with competence, as follows:

> One purpose of this paper is to argue that underpinning knowledge is such an important aspect of many jobs that its omission will lead to seriously inadequate descriptions of performance. Another is to advocate approaches to functional analysis which take into account the probability

of there being significant underpinning knowledge. (Eraut, 1990, in Black and Wolf, p 22)

The importance of knowledge and understanding seems clearer at the higher levels of the NVQs, in management education, for example, where the idea of a polarization of academic knowledge and vocational competence seems misguided. There needs to be a close relationship between academic competence and vocational competence, as Leigh explains:

> The key . . . must be acceptance that academic study and achievement has value, not just at the individual level, but to the corporate world. In effect, there is such a thing as academic competence which underpins occupational competence. [This view] corresponds to the NCVQ's insistence that underpinning 'knowledge and understanding' is something which should be assessed. Indeed, this is the site where academic and vocational sides have a natural conjuncture. The acceptance that competence is maintained over a long period by knowledge of methods, principles, etc, is something which continues to require attention. (Leigh, 1992, p 19)

This 'natural conjuncture' is an important issue to stress as we examine the various aims of education and training and the meanings of 'learning'. So both academic and vocational competence are needed as the outcomes of education and training programmes.

The EHE initiative is attempting to stimulate change and innovation in UK universities and polytechnics by introducing 'enterprise' to the debates about teaching and learning. Despite the strong ideological overtones of the term 'enterprise', particularly during the Thatcherite period, the higher education institutions participating in the scheme have evolved their own definitions and meanings for it. These definitions have placed 'skills' at the centre stage of the debate. Three broad definitions have been adopted, as follows:

> The Entrepreneurial – concerned with developing skills useful in the business world.
> The Employer Link – concerned with students' projects and placements with employers in a 'real economic setting'.
> The Personal Transferable Skills – concerned with generic personal competencies seen as relevant to the world of work and elsewhere. (Tavistock Institute of Human Relations, 1990, p 11)

More recently 'enterprise' in the EHE scheme has become recognized as concerned with the broader skills of adult learning, as follows: 'Helping students to become effective lifelong learners so that they are equipped for their future working lives' (Brown, 1991, p 11).

If we are to help students develop as learners and facilitate them in learning to learn, it seems clear that we need to pay far more attention to how our learners perceive learning. Learning has such a central position in education and training, it is essential that we try to understand more about learning from the learner's perspective. At the same time, we need to help students to become more aware of their own views about learning.

In looking at 'learning' in a broad sense, I have introduced this current work from the vocational sector, as I think it shows the shortcomings of the academic/vocational divide. Also, although much of the research discussed in this book has been carried out with students engaged in degree level studies, I want to situate this research in the wider context of student learning. Just as the NCVQ is committed to the importance of academic knowledge underpinning competence, we can see the need for this if we look at what students do in some of their learning activities; it is possible for certain activities to be performed (competence at one level), but with little understanding of the underlying rationale. We shall look these issues in more detail in Chapter 4.

What I want to establish is that any reforming or restructuring of education and training requires us to look critically at our teaching and learning, that is to theorize our practice. By implication then in this process, we are looking at various conceptions of learning in particular areas held by the teachers or trainers responsible to professional bodies. In improving students' learning, we also need to understand more about how students perceive learning.

Students' views of learning

I never really thought about what studying was or what learning was. I mean I'd had years of it at school and now I was going to have a few more years in college. Like being on a conveyor belt really – you're too busy rolling along and keeping on top of things to worry what it's all about. Pity really, to think what I could have made of my chances if I'd been more clued up. (Rowntree, 1988, p 8)

This type of remark is not uncommon when students are interviewed about their experiences of college. Although this student had passed the course and was looking back at the end of three years, there was certainly a feeling that study after school could somehow be more rewarding. This student was successful at one level, in terms of the grades to pass the course, but seemed to pass through the educational system in a totally unreflective way, 'like being on a conveyor belt'.

How is it that this student described studying in such a dismal manner? There is some suggestion that going to college was the next step on the ladder from school. In terms of the concept of orientation to education discussed in Chapter 2, this could be interpreted as an 'academic extrinsic orientation'. Another important issue is the taken-for-granted, unreflective way in which learning is described.

If we return to the title of this chapter, 'What is learning?', why is it so important to address this question? As teachers and course designers we often do not appreciate the complexity of the concept of 'learning', and we fail to understand that many of our students hold quite different views about what learning actually is. This concern is not just an academic educational research question, far from it. For student learning, it has a crucial influence on how they tackle their work. It is partly the pervasiveness of 'learning' that contributes to its 'taken-for-granted' nature. Most students engaged in education and training will have some recollections of the sort of learning they experienced at school level in compulsory education. For the student quoted above, the school experience seemed to have continued through college.

It is also likely that students will have seen various television quiz programmes, which convey a particular view of learning. In the UK, for example, quiz shows such as *Mastermind* and *University Challenge* require the participants to know a large amount of factual material which has to be recalled very rapidly. Superficially, such quiz games seem impressive. However, very rarely do the questions ask for any form of explanation, the questions merely have right or wrong answers. This presentation of factual knowledge does not require understanding or the bringing together of ideas to address a new problem or question.

The taken-for-granted nature of learning then conceals the issue that many students, particularly those in the early stages of their careers as learners, have very different and far less sophisticated conceptions of learning than we have as teachers, trainers and course writers. The conceptions of learning which our students hold vitally affect how they tackle a particular learning task.

Students understand the tasks facing them in different ways. When a teacher gives a lecture she will probably assume that the purpose of the lecture is perfectly clear, and that the task facing students attending the lecture is both obvious and shared by all those attending. In practice this is not the case. In fact it seems to be quite common both for students to have very different perceptions of the purposes of the lecture from that of the lecturer, and for students to differ from each other in their perceptions. These differences directly affect what students do during lectures, so that they may end up doing something which the lecturer could not have predicted and which she might find rather odd. Although for the majority of students engaged in open and distance learning a full series of lectures is unlikely to be part of the teaching, there will almost certainly be some face-to-face sessions in the form of lectures, probably intended to convey new information or consolidate difficult aspects of a course. The 'lecture format' or 'traditional teaching' is likely to be at least one component of almost any education and training course. The ways in which students respond in a lecture are pivotal in all sectors of training and education. Let us look at an example.

With a colleague, I was once asked by a politics lecturer to help improve the note-taking skills of his students. We were to be allowed five minutes at the end of a lecture in which to do this. We attended the whole lecture, took notes, and also tried to observe what the students were doing. It became clear that they were writing notes when we were just listening, and listening when we were taking notes. We were obviously writing different things down, and probably therefore found different things important. Perhaps they simply understood the subject better than we did. But as time went on it became clear that they were writing down detailed information, dates, names and all sorts of factual information, while we were not. Sometimes the lecturer turned from writing information on the blackboard and made a general theoretical statement (eg 'So it can be seen how A's ideas on social change differed from those of B's, etc, and how their respective political and social contexts help to explain these differences of view'). Many of the students seemed to have completely ignored such statements, or else did not know what to do with them. Some of them appeared to have put their pens down and waited until the lecturer reverted to describing further political and historical details before resuming note-taking. Sometimes the lecturer even said things like: 'Now the really important thing here is . . . ' and would then outline an abstract or general point which pulled together the previous section of the lecture. Many students ignored these too. Their notes appeared to consist of chronological lists of events, and abstract overviews had little place in their neat lists.

In the last five minutes we asked all the students: 'What were the three most important things in this lecture? If you took nothing else away with you from this lecture than three points, what would these points be? Please write them down.' We asked the lecturer to do the same thing, and to write his points on an overhead projector transparency so they could be projected to the group. When we displayed the lecturer's three points, we found that out of sixty students, none had written down all three of these points. About twenty had written down one or two of them. It was clear that what the lecturer thought was important, and should have been learnt, was not perceived as important by the students. In fact the students had found great difficulty in deciding what three points were most important. Their notes were more mainly in the form of large amounts of information indistinguishable in their relative importance.

This politics lecturer was able to see that it was not students' note-taking 'techniques' which were at fault. Their problem was that their attention was focused on the wrong aspects of the lecture. They understood the task facing them in attending the lecture in a way which did not match up to his intentions.

In working with students to help them recognize what sort of demands different lecturers make, the following caricatures have been used effectively:

> Dr Tort expects her students to learn legal principles from books and to apply those principles to specific cases in the seminars. In her law lectures she demonstrates how to apply principles to cases. She is 'modelling' by lecturing, saying 'I want you to be able to do it like this'.

> Mr Spanner gives mechanics lectures as a way of delivering course material to his students. He is expecting them to copy from the blackboard everything that he writes there. He is copying from his notes. His notes are copied from textbooks which are available in the library and in the bookshops. His lectures give students selected extracts, with some commentary, from these books.

> Dr Group talks about the sociology of groups in his lectures. The books (and there are twenty on his reading list for each lecture and hundreds in the library) all seem somewhat tangential to the topic. They all use special terminology and are difficult to make sense of. The lecture is a guide to a strange land. Dr Group gives students a map, indicates landmarks to look out for, and points out a few things about this strange land which they might have trouble finding on their own. He gives them a tourist's smattering of the language they will need in this land. He is trying to prevent them from getting lost when they start reading.

> Mr System tells students the five elements of personnel management in his lecture. Each element has five sub-elements, and he gives an example of each. He is going to test students to see whether they can list these elements and give examples. His lectures are the content of the course. If students take a full set of notes and memorize them, they will pass the course.

> Dr Engels tries to explain dialectical materialism in her lecture. It is a difficult idea to grasp. She uses illustrations and metaphors. She repeats herself. She accepts questions from students. She uses every

device she can think of to get the concept across. She doesn't care whether students take any notes or not as long as they understand dialectical materialism better than they did before. (Habeshaw, Habeshaw and Gibbs, 1987, pp 93–4)

Students can be asked to think of one of their own lecturers and to try to identify which caricature he or she is closest to. Having done that, students can then go on to explore what would be a sensible thing to try to do, when they are in that person's lectures.

The politics lecturer described above was operating as a Mr Group and Dr Engels combined; he presented several key ideas in a way that would make the subsequent reading of set historical texts a little easier and more rewarding. However, the students clearly saw the lecturer as a Mr System: a rather unstructured Mr System perhaps, but nevertheless as a lecturer who presented a body of information to be reproduced. When the lecturer fitted in with this perception and actually presented factual information they responded by writing it all down in their notes. When he departed from their perception and became more discursive, exploratory and analytical, they tended to be confused, and did nothing, simply waiting for the next bit of information to come along.

It might be argued that students only make these sorts of mistakes, and hold these misconceptions, while they are inexperienced, and before they have encountered a wider variety of teaching situations. To an extent this is the case. Students do become more sophisticated over time in their ability to respond appropriately to different task demands in study situations. However, underlying students' perceptions are more pervasive and deep-rooted factors than their mere experience of a range of different situations. It is not simply students' understanding of lectures which develops through experience; their understanding of learning itself also develops over time. Their experience of different styles of lecture may gradually bring about changes in their understanding of learning. But their understanding of learning may also be seen as a constraint, limiting the scope of students' perceptions of lectures, and leading to the sort of behaviour we observed in the politics lecture outlined above.

Although for many students in open and distance learning, lectures are likely to be a relatively infrequent occurrence, the importance of the underlying perceptions of learning will pervade throughout their studies. So, although the bulk of the teaching is presented through the textual medium, the same issues of what students are expected to do with the materials will apply.

Investigating conceptions of learning

The next part of this chapter is concerned with what people understand learning to be about, and how this understanding develops and changes over time. The way in which students perceive learning is a fundamental tenet in all education and training. The research to explore students' conceptions of learning has used individual in-depth interviews to get students to talk about their own learning and to elaborate it with examples. The following questions are examples of the key questions which have been asked in this research. (See for example, Säljö, 1982.)

- What do you understand by learning?
- What do you mean by learning?
- What is involved when you come to learn something?
- What exactly do you mean by learning?

When we asked students this last question, they answered in ways which differed in important and interesting respects (Morgan, Gibbs and Taylor, 1981) Take the following examples:

Interviewer	Can I ask you, what do you mean by learning? When you think of learning something, what does it mean to you?
Student	To gain some knowledge, I think is learning. We're learning all the time, not necessarily by sitting down and studying. I think there are all kinds of ways. But to me learning is gaining knowledge.
Interviewer	Can you explain what you mean by gaining knowledge?
Student	I suppose just picking up bits of information really - I think if you do it, quite basically that's what it is. We do that every day in our life – perhaps do it to a greater degree by doing a course. We obviously want to learn more. I obviously want more knowledge about things and I've got an interest in things and I want to know as much as possible about them.
Interviewer	So it is gaining pieces of knowledge?
Student	Yes, yes.

Contrast this first example with what this second student said:

Interviewer	When you say learning, what does learning mean to you? What do you mean by learning?
Student	Understanding, I think. Understanding, you can read it, that's OK, and memorize it, but unless you understand

the reason that a thing . . . is what it is and why it is . . .
it's not worth it, you haven't learnt a thing. You've got to
gain like an experience from reading it and you know
. . . totally experience it. I think any kind of learning is
going to have to change you. If you do really learn. With
social science you learn to understand about people and
the world about you and why things happen, and therefore when you understand more why they happen, it
changes you, your attitudes to everything . . . It must
affect your everyday beliefs – It's got to.

These two students had just started their first year with the OU, studying the
same social science course. One would expect these two students to
approach the learning tasks they would tackle on their course in quite different
ways because they hold such different views as to what learning consists of.
It is not the case that these are two different sorts of people, for example,
that the second student is 'brighter' or 'more motivated' than the first one.
Rather they are at different stages in their development as learners, a development that we all go through. A third student when asked the question:
'What exactly do you mean by learning?' at the start of her first year, replied
in much the same way as the first student above. But by the middle of her
second year she had quite a different response, as follows:

Well obviously it isn't learning facts and figures in this course. There
is an amount of learning facts and figures but basically I think of it
more as understanding the different issues that are brought up . . .
because there aren't any hard facts to learn, there are always so many
different sides. So it isn't so much learning, as understanding the problems and the facts that affect the final decision, because there isn't
really a 'right' and a 'wrong', it depends who you are. Learning, as we
are being taught now, is meant as understanding, rather than learning
facts by memory.

By this point she was able to distinguish between learning as the accumulation
or memorization of facts and learning as understanding. She had yet to
develop the very personal conception of learning expressed by the second
student above, in which learning is seen as changing oneself and one's perception of the everyday world.

This development over time is further illustrated with a fourth student,
interviewed four times over a period of three years. At the start of her first
course she was asked:

Interviewer   When you say learning, what exactly do you mean by
learning?

Mrs D   Well, I don't know really. I suppose knowing things that
         I don't know about. When I do think of learning it is still
         very much a school sort of thing, the facts and dates and
         names learning rather than content. And if I read some-
         thing I'm so bored about taking in what it says that I have
         read it and I think 'what have I just read?' . . . I don't
         even know who wrote it or what it was about and I think
         at the moment I feel worried about not taking in what I
         am doing or what I am learning.

By the end of her first year of studying Mrs D had developed some study
techniques to cope with the course. She was more organized, and took more
notes. However, she still understood learning to mean 'taking things in' or
memorizing:

Well – I think of learning, when it comes to revision time – I'll have a
list of names to remember.

A year later her response to the same question was quite different:

Well I can't remember whatever I said last time, but for me now if this
is learning, then it gives me a new awareness. I just look further into
things and maybe think a bit more, and think of the other person's
point of view when somebody or other says something or: 'Who said
it? and 'Who are they to say it?' and 'Why should we take any notice
of what they are saying?' Learning is just more of an awareness.

And a further year on, two-and-a-half years after her response in the first
interview, above, she said:

Well, I don't know really. But, I'm a lot more bolshy than I've ever
been . . . somehow I feel more aware of everything that's going on
around me. Certainly far more aware of myself, particularly the
woman aware of myself. I found that this has grown with being with
the OU, nothing to do directly with the contents of what I've been
doing. There just seems to be more of an awareness in me, I'm going
through a stage.

From seeing the learning task as involving the memorization of factual information her course presented to her, she had become first critical of information
and views presented by others, and then more aware of her own position in a
very personal way. She even describes herself, after two-and-a-half years'
studying, as 'going through a stage'.

The way students describe their conception of learning is influenced by
their reasons for wanting to study. Furthermore their way of actually going

about study tasks can be limited by their conception of learning. These links will be explored further in Chapter 4. Here I shall focus on the frameworks which are available to make sense of the sorts of differences and developments in students' conceptions of learning which the above students have illustrated.

So far, I have only presented examples from four students. However, these variations have been developed into a more general framework from interviews with a large number of students. This framework distinguishes between six different conceptions of learning. Although the examples mentioned so far are from university-level students, similar issues of conceptions of learning have been identified with trainee engineering technicians (Strang, 1987).

Students' conceptions of learning

The research of Roger Säljö (1982) has identified five distinct conceptions of learning. These five qualitatively different conceptions can be summarized as follows:

1. Learning as the increase of knowledge
The main feature of this category is its vagueness in that answers to the question, 'What does learning mean to you?' were merely synonyms of word learning: 'It's to increase your knowledge – well you kind of start with a small bag and there's not much in it, but then the longer you live, the more you will fill it up.'

The first example presented above falls within this category. There is no notion of how this gaining of information occurs or to what purpose it is undertaken.

2. Learning as memorizing
This conception of learning is characterized as follows: 'The meaning of learning is to transfer units of information or knowledge, or what is commonly referred to simply as facts, from an external source such as a teacher or a book, into the head.' 'To learn, well, as I understand the word, to listen to and get it inside your head, acquire knowledge . . . simply to learn it to get things in one's head so they stay there.'

3. Learning as the acquisition of facts, procedures, etc, which can be retained and/or utilized in practice
Compared to the previous conceptions, in this case, facts, principles and procedures, etc, are considered to be practically useful and should be remembered for a long time, and as a consequence of this they should be

learned. 'It shouldn't be just learning something which disappears imme-
diately after you've learned it, but you should be able to make use of it.'

Although there is some distinction about learning, it should be something
useful, there is no mention of understanding issues or changing the way
things are understood.

4. Learning as the abstraction of meaning

In contrast to the previous categories, the main characteristic of this conception
is that the nature of what is learned is changed. Learning is no longer conceived of as an activity of reproducing information, but rather as a process of
abstracting meaning from what is read or listened to. For example, 'for me
personally, learning does not mean that you should learn all those petty
details, but instead it means learning about a course of events and how things
have developed, and reasoning within the subject, but it does not mean sit-
ting and memorizing trifles such as dates and facts, etc.'

The notion that learning is only concerned with memorizing and reproducing information is replaced by a conception which emphasizes that learning
is a constructive activity. The learning material is not viewed as presenting
'ready-made' knowledge to be memorized. This conception involves the student
as an active agent, but what is learnt is not necessarily of personal significance. The emphasis is primarily on understanding existing work and other
people's ideas and theories, rather than developing one's own.

5. Learning as an interpretative process aimed at the understanding of some personal reality

This conception is very similar to the previous one, with the emphasis on
constructing meaning. However, the distinction is that in many subject areas
a key part of learning is that the learners interpret the realities in which they
live. For example, 'learning means to get the sort of insights into your subject so that you can use them in your everyday life.'

So to summarize these variations in conceptions of learning, essentially
Säljö's conceptions 1, 2 and 3 are concerned with learning as memorizing
and reproducing information, whereas conceptions 4 and 5 are concerned
with constructing meaning and transformation and 'going beyond the information given'. Although Säljö identified these various conceptions of learning with different groups of learners, there seems to be clear developmental
implication in his work.

There are many parallels in the work on conception of learning and the
research of William Perry (1970). The strength of Perry's work is that it is
based on a longitudinal study of students over a period of four years. He
documented the changes students progressed through, identifying nine
stages. These nine stages can be summarized into three very clear distinctions, representing the different ways students viewed their studies. Students

initially saw learning in absolutist terms: there are right and wrong answers to questions. Students then progressed to seeing learning in more relativistic terms, and finally some students moved to having a personal commitment to a particular perspective within this framework. The following extract from Perry's work demonstrates these different stages of development.

> Let us suppose that a lecturer announces that today he will consider three theories explanatory of – (whatever his topic may be). Student A has always taken it for granted that knowledge consists of correct answers, that there is one right answer per problem, and that teachers explain these answers for students to learn. He therefore listens for the lecturer to state which theory he is to learn.
>
> Student B makes the same general assumptions but with an elaboration to the effect that teachers sometimes present problems and procedures, rather then answers, 'so that we can learn to find the right answer on our own.' He therefore perceives the lecture as a kind of guessing game in which he has to 'figure out' which theory is correct, a game which is fair enough if the lecturer does not carry it so far as to hide things too obscurely.
>
> Student C assumes that an answer can be called 'right' only in the light of its context, and that contexts or 'frames of reference' differ. He assumes that several interpretations of a poem, explanations of a historical development, or even theories of a class of events in physics may be legitimate 'depending on how you look at it.' Though he feels a little uneasy in such a kaleidoscopic world, he nonetheless supposes that the lecturer may be about to present three legitimate theories which can be examined for their internal coherence, their scope, their fit with various data, their predictive power, etc.
>
> Whatever the lecturer then proceeds to do (in terms of his own assumptions and intent) these three students will make meaning of the experience in different ways which all involve different assessments of their own choices and responsibilities. (Perry, 1970, p 2)

In Perry's hypothetical lecture, if we assume that the three students A, B and C are the same person at different times in a learner's time in college or following a course, we can see the notion of 'stages of development'. Perry's work is important in that it describes how students change over time. Although there the focus is on development and growth, Perry also identified 'regression', where the learner failed to progress and moved back to earlier stages in his or her development.

Perry only studied students in Harvard and Radcliffe colleges in the USA, with a relatively homogeneous student population, and has been criticized for concentrating on middle-class male students, (Belenky et al, 1986). However, his work is still valuable as it provides a basis for reflection on education and training in a wide range of settings, although specific issues of women's intellectual development are not included. As teachers, trainers and course designers, what are the assumptions about the nature of learning embodied in our teaching? How do we want our students to engage with the discourse of our teaching?

Recent work on conceptions of learning has identified a further conception about 'changing as a person - a fundamental change about seeing oneself and a way of seeing what is learnt' (Marton et al, 1992). This can be seen as an 'extension' of the Säljö level 5. This further conception of learning, Level 6, is again concerned with 'transformation', but the emphasis is on personal change and development. Learning as a change in this sense of seeing oneself differently is often described by adult mature students. Although they were initially engaged in study for the content of a particular course, during the process of study other issues besides content can come into the foreground.

As we saw earlier, the way in which students perceive learning influences what they actually do when tackling a particular piece of work. This work could be listening and note-taking in a lecture (the example above), or it could be working with a self-study correspondence text or preparing an assignment for an open learning course for accreditation by some professional body. Students' conceptions of learning have almost a 'limiting' influence on how they approach their study activities. This is taken up further in Chapter 4.

Although much of this research has been conducted in formal educational settings, where students have been engaged in academic types of study, and in the case of Perry (1970) with a homogeneous group of students, similar variations in perceptions of learning have been identified with Open Tech students in the UK (Strang, 1987). In this study Strang interviewed students on a range of Open Tech courses about their experiences of study, how they tackled their work and also asked them questions to explore their conceptions of learning. Here is how one of the interviewees, Derek, who was following a course on maintenance and repair of agricultural equipment answered the question, 'What do you actually mean by learning?': 'I guess it means remembering what you've just read.' (Strang, 1987, p 38). In terms of Säljö's scheme, this can be interpreted as Level 2. A range of conceptions of learning were identified with these Open Tech students and it was concluded that the notion of 'conception of learning' is also useful for understanding learning in technical and vocational settings.

Conclusion

So, as teachers, trainers and course designers, what are we to do about students' conceptions of learning? How do they help us to refine our implicit theories of learning, which tend to guide our work as practitioners? First, there is a clear message that we need to adopt holistic models of the learner in our discussions and debates about how to help students. Second, students need to become more aware of how they perceive learning, as a precursor to changing their own awareness of what learning itself consists of. How can we do this in open and distance learning? Clearly face-to-face interactions, where there is the scope for dialogue between learners and teachers can be valuable. The example of the various caricatures of lecturers outlined above, as provided by Habeshaw, Habeshaw and Gibbs (1987) can be used with students to help them become more aware of lecturers' assumptions about what is required of them as learners. However, even where students are studying at a distance, with relatively little opportunity for face-to-face interaction, both correspondence text and assessment can be designed to enhance dialogue. In fact Evans and Nation (1989a) place dialogue at the centre of all teaching and learning. The aim is to help students to become more aware of the range of purposes and assumptions embodied in an open learning text. Although the text medium, combined with a high quality presentation, may tend to emphasize 'transmission modes' of teaching, we need to adopt assessment strategies which encourage students to interact with and to question the material presented to them. Again in terms of helping students, the aim is to enable learning to become 'thematized', in the words of Roger Säljö; that is learning itself becomes an issue for conscious reflection. In Chapter 5, we shall look at some examples of how assessment has been used creatively to help students to become more aware of their own learning. With these steps, we should be able to help students to develop as learners, to go beyond the 'taken for granted' notion of learning or 'being on a conveyor belt', to experience learning as something which 'engages them in a personally meaningful way', to use the words of Rogers (1969).

Chapter 4
How do students go about their studies?

Introduction

How do students go about their studies? What processes do learners engage in when they 'really' come to understand something? This Chapter looks at the different ways in which students describe their studying. What students actually do when they are attempting to learn and understand is of vital importance, as this has a direct influence on the quality of the learning outcomes. The different ways in which students go about study have been identified in a range of educational settings and they seem relevant to education and training in a wide context. To put this more formally, qualitatively different 'approaches to learning' have been identified with students engaged in a wide range of learning activities.

Learning and understanding in everyday contexts

I want to illuminate what is involved when a person 'really comes to understand' something by looking at examples from everyday contexts. Although these examples may seem somewhat outside the realms of training and education, I think we can gain insights from them. When we talk about learning something, we may say, 'Ah – now I see what it is about. Now I get it,' or use the colloquial expression 'the penny drops' as at last we begin to understand. What is involved when 'the penny drops' and understanding occurs?

Consider attempting to find your way around an entirely strange town or city in which you have just arrived by aeroplane. Although you may have a map, you are initially confronted with an apparently unconnected and confusing set of roads, streets and freeways. You are only able to find your way around by frequent reference to the map. However, in time the individual parts and components of this jigsaw, the streets, pedestrian ways, etc, are viewed in a different relation to one another to constitute a new 'whole picture' to represent the area. The same information and detail is viewed as a new 'gestalt' – a new whole, and it is not possible to revert to seeing things in the original confused fashion. The point is that this process requires a change in awareness in the relationships between various pieces of information.

Let us look at another example of finding one's way around a strange city, driving a car. I shall describe driving around a strange city and making sense of the traffic regulations and road layouts. Here is how I found my first experience of driving around the centre of Melbourne, Australia.

As we approached the centre of the city, my Australian passenger, who was also acting as navigator, began to describe the route and specifically a right turn that we would be taking in a few minutes. He explained:

'It's one of those "funny right turns" where you can only turn right from the left hand lane.'

'I don't believe you,' I replied, thinking that this was some sort of Australian joke designed to confuse European visitors.

I continued driving, somewhat apprehensively now. The experience of twenty years driving in Britain (Australia also drives on the left-hand side) suddenly did not look quite so useful. I was still convinced that the idea of turning right from the left-hand lane was a joke. As we approached the junction, my Australian passenger said he would tell me what to do, just follow my directions! In the busy main street with numerous vehicles, pedestrians and also trams, traffic lights and signposts, there was little else I could do. There was no time for further discussion!

'OK. Here we come; just signal right and pull over to the left-hand lane and wait there. When the traffic lights turn yellow, make a bit of a dash across to the right. And oh, watch out for the trams as well!'

Still in a sense of total confusion and amazement, I followed the directions rigorously. I completed the manoeuvre successfully but with total ignorance of any rationale for the procedure, especially when it was entirely contrary to my other driving experiences.

Subsequent discussion helped my understanding. The relatively narrow main street in the city has trams running along the centre. There is not sufficient space for motor vehicles to wait in the centre of the street without blocking the tram lines, so the vehicles waiting to turn right queue on the left hand side in a lane where the pavement has been moved back to create an extra lane just by the junction. When the traffic going straight-on at the junction is stopped by the traffic lights, the vehicles waiting to turn right can then proceed from the queuing lane for the right turn, which is located on the far left-hand side of the street. It may appear a strange procedure, but seems to be the only way to fit in demands on the space of the tramlines, roadway and pavements, without totally redesigning the street. (There are actually six junctions with this 'peculiar' layout on the main street of Melbourne, where the space is very restricted.) The layout of 'funny right turn' is set out in Figure 1.

'So that's the reason! Now I am starting to understand what is required of me in these funny right turns.'

A transformation, a change of awareness on my part was required before the demands of this driving manoeuvre could be comprehended. I had to reflect on the information, the details of the road layout, the position of the tramlines, etc, and to re-order it before I was able to understand the basis for the 'funny right turns'.

This example shows how it is possible to carry out a set of procedures without understanding the rationale for it. Similarly with instruction manuals

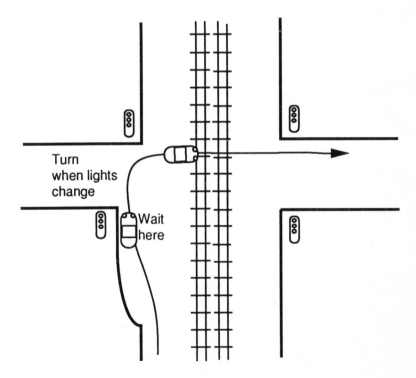

Figure 1 *Understanding 'funny right turns'*

for many consumer goods, you may well have had your own experiences of struggling to 'figure out' what is meant by a set of directions or instructions without understanding the principles involved.

What relevance do these examples have for student learning? Similar sorts of transformations seem to be a key part of students coming to understand new material. Finding just what is really required and the rationale for it is an important part of students' experiences.

In the simple example of driving, for me to 'really understand' the underlying rationale, I think it required a sort of 'destructuring' of the experience and information followed by a 'restructuring' in my own terms, which helped me to make sense of this simple procedure of turning right.

Of course, my everyday example of learning and understanding is very simple. However, I think it shows vividly how it is possible to carry out a set of procedures, but to lack any understanding of the underlying rationale. In Chapter 3, we looked briefly at some of the issues in the knowledge and competence debate and the assessment of performance. Both in the case of the 'funny right turns' in Melbourne and in various instruction manuals, it is possible to perform a task competently, but without any understanding of the knowledge which underlies the particular competence.

I think these examples can help us to get insights into what students have to be engaged in for them to 'really understand something'. Also everyday examples of learning can be discussed with students to help them become more aware of their own studying when engaged in more conventional learning tasks in education and training. These actual processes of learning extend and build upon the framework of students' conceptions of learning set out in Chapter 3. Although the examples above of understanding in everyday contexts are simple cases, similar issues are involved in the way students describe their studies. I now want to look in detail at students' approaches to learning.

Students' approaches to learning

How do students describe their own efforts as they grapple with their work for an assignment or perhaps prepare themselves for an examination? Here is one student talking about studying:

> I didn't think about this problem. I just bashed the numbers out. I went straight through it without looking back at anything. I wasn't interested but well you've got to do this stuff. In this sort of problem you've just got to get through to the answer. I find it pretty dull doing it this way so I don't spend long on it. I've got these notes from the

lectures. These ones aren't too bad, but you often miss things, and can't make head or tail of them afterwards. You don't need to read books . . . provided you get it all down you can't go wrong. It's getting it all down that's the problem. But here it was OK. You just have to more or less get the right formula and bung the figures in. (Gibbs, Morgan and Taylor, 1982, p 10)

A number of key features stand out in this student's interview. First, the student's task in lectures is perceived as 'getting it all down'. Second, there was a general lack of interest in doing the assignment, it appeared to be forced on the student as a demand of the assessment system. Third, the study pattern is one of 'bashing out the numbers without looking back at anything.' And fourth, the approach to doing the assignment was to 'get the right formula and bung in the numbers'. There are parallels between this final point about 'getting the right formula' and the examples of learning in everyday settings above, where it is possible to carry out a procedure without any understanding of the underlying rationale. The lack of reflectiveness in tackling the work and its assessment-driven nature can be interpreted as a 'surface approach' to learning.

'Approach to learning' is one of the key concepts for understanding how students are tackling their studies. The major distinction identified by Marton and Säljö (1976) is between a deep approach and a surface approach to learning. The original studies of Marton and Säljö (1976) focused on the study of academic articles. What is so important about this research is that the learners were engaged in tasks which were relevant to their normal studies. The research subjects studied 3000-word articles, on topics they were likely to meet later in the course of their normal studies, in contrast to much of the research on learning from text which has focused on a single page of text or even a few paragraphs. Besides the validity of the learning activities, Marton and Säljö (1976) also used valid measures of learning outcomes (these are discussed in Chapter 6).

The basic methodological approach of all the research discussed in this book is to enable learners to describe their experiences from their own perspectives, thus the individual in-depth interview has been the predominant research method. So to find out how students tackled various learning activities, they were asked questions such as:

Could you describe how you went about reading the text?
Was there anything you found difficult?
Did you find it interesting or not?
While reading, was there anything that struck you as particularly important? (Marton and Säljö, 1984, p 38)

The analysis of the interview transcripts revealed two very different ways in which students decribed how they had gone about the learning task. The different ways of attempting to learn from the text were labelled as surface and deep-level processing. Although 'levels of processing' was the term used in the original research, the research has been extended to include normal studies, and the distinction between deep and surface 'approaches to learning' has been used.

Approaches to learning describe what students do when engaged in studying textual materials. Learners focus their attention in quite different ways; on one hand they concentrate on memorizing facts and details (a surface approach), in contrast to searching for meaning and the overall message the author is trying to convey (a deep approach). The importance of the approach to learning is that it is directly linked to the quality of the learning outcomes. Students who take a surface approach fail to gain a good grasp of the content of their readings, whereas those who take a deep approach to learning do gain a full understanding of the issues in question.

The original studies of Marton and Säljö (1976) have been extended and developed to include a wide range of learning contexts, such as doing assignments, problem solving in science, learning from lectures as well as studying in distance education (for a summary of this work see Marton, Hounsell and Entwistle, 1984)

Ramsden (1988) draws together the slightly different ways in which approaches to learning have been described and provides a useful summary, as follows:

Deep approach

Intention to understand
Focus on what 'is signified' (eg the author's arguments)
Relate and distinguish new ideas and previous knowledge
Relate concepts to everyday experience
Organize and structure content
Internal emphasis: 'A window through which aspects of reality become visible, and more intelligible'

Surface approach

Intention to complete [learning] task requirements
Focus on the 'signs' (eg the text itself)
Focus on discrete elements
Memorize information and procedures for assessment
Unreflectively associate concepts and facts

Fail to distinguish principles from evidence, new information from old
Treat [learning] task as an external imposition
External emphasis: demands of assessment, knowledge cut off from
everyday reality (Ramsden, 1988, p 19).

From this summary, we can see that my descriptions of 'following procedures', in the everyday example of learning at the beginning of this Chapter, can be interpreted as a sort of 'surface approach'. Attention was directed only at completing the task without any broader considerations. When I started to 'really understand' what was involved, I had to re-order and restructure the information presented.

Before we move on to look at approaches to learning more specifically in the context of open and distance learning, there are two further important aspects of students' approaches to learning. There is a strategic aspect of how students go about their studies and also the context specificity about how they tackle their studies.

Entwistle and Ramsden (1983) identified what they termed a 'strategic approach to study', where students are concerned to get the best grade possible and this may involve both a surface approach and a deep approach to learning, depending on the nature of the task. There are parallels here to the work of Miller and Parlett (1974) who identified 'cue-consciousness' as an important aspect of how students negotiate the assessment system. (This role of assessment in learning is discussed further in Chapter 5.) Also Lockwood (1992) has extended the concept of 'cue-consciousness' to a more specific idea of 'assignment-focus' to describe the different ways in which students go about their work in open and distance learning.

The context specificity and the role of assessment in influencing students' approaches to learning is one of the key findings of the research of Laurillard (1979), who found that an assignment was tackled differently depending on how a student perceived its importance and interest. Hence the notion of variability in students' approaches to learning. Although in Chapter 3 we have seen how some students appeared to be constrained in their studies by their conception of learning, all students have the potential to engage in 'personally meaningful' learning of the form described by Carl Rogers (1969). It is incorrect to 'label' individual students as deep or surface learners. Although there will be some consistency in how students tackle their studies, a type of habitual response to study, the detailed context of the particular course or assignment will have an overriding influence. As teachers, trainers and course designers, the challenge for us in improving learning is to help facilitate students to take a deep approach to learning, by adopting particular approaches to course design and assessment.

Recent research by Entwistle and Entwistle (1992) provides insights into approaches to learning and understanding. They set out to explore how students perceived 'understanding' by interviewing a group of students just after they had completed their final examinations. Students were asked about 'what they believed understanding to involve' in terms of their own experience, how they developed and checked their understanding of topics, and what they did when the material proved difficult to understand. Although the student sample in this study was rather biased (predominantly very successful ones), it provides useful insights into the process involved in understanding. For students in open and distance learning, although they are studying in a very different social context from the majority of conventional-age campus-based students, the detailed processes through which people come to understand concepts, ideas and aspects of reality seem to be very similar.

Students interviewed by Entwistle and Entwistle described the nature of understanding to be concerned with the notions of seeing a whole and coherence in an area of study, and also an emotional dimension of feelings of satisfaction.

> Students repeatedly commented that the experience of understanding generally had a feeling tone associated with it – there was necessarily an emotional response, at least where significant understanding had been achieved. The inseparability of cognitive and emotional components of understanding was very clear in the comments made by the students. Within our sample, understanding was experienced as a feeling of satisfaction although that feeling varied in its expression from the sudden 'aha', as confusion on a particular topic was replaced by insight, to a less dramatic feeling associated either with being able to follow a lecture or with an emerging appreciation of the nature of the discipline itself. This feeling was derived from a recognition of the meaning and significance of the material learned, and on occasions had its origins in previous personal or professional experience. (Entwistle and Entwistle 1992, p7)

In terms of the processes which students were engaged in as they came to gain these understandings, there are parallels to the key features of a deep approach to learning. Students described their study as being concerned with active engagement with course books and lectures, and attempting to construct meaning from the diversity of sources.

> Understanding was essentially an active process which involved relating new ideas to what was already known, examining evidence and the logic of the material, and creating an integrated whole. Where the material was initially difficult, the development of understanding

required an active engagement with the material being learned, involving internal debates about the new material and its meaning, or discussions with friends. Several students talked about the importance they attached to discussion in the process of developing understanding. In some instances they would talk to a tutor or a more senior student, but they often preferred to engage in debate with other students in their year. Several students commented on the value they found in discussing their own understanding with others, and how this had led to a clarification of their own ideas. (Entwistle and Entwistle, 1992, p 10)

In terms of improving learning so as to enhance understanding, it seems to be well established that we need to help students to become involved in various forms of 'dialogue', so as to enable them to become more actively involved with material and to help them relate it to previous knowledge and personal experience.

Although the research we have discussed so far in this Chapter has been carried out with students in conventional educational settings, it is directly relevant in open learning and distance education. The detailed processes of learning which are required for students to gain a full understanding are very similar. Also with the current changes in all forms of post-compulsory education, where self-instructional or open learning materials are increasingly being used in a variety of ways, there seems to be a sort of 'coalescence' of open and distance learning and learning in conventional settings. In the next section studies carried out in open and distance learning will be looked at in detail.

Approaches in open learning and distance education

How does the concept of 'approach to learning' relate to students engaged in open learning and distance education? Is the concept relevant for students engaged in education and training and for adult learners? The research done with OU students (mature adults) studying social sciences and also those studying technology, indicates the significance of the 'approach to learning' in open and distance learning (Morgan, Taylor, and Gibbs, 1982; Morgan, Gibbs, and Taylor, 1980). With students engaged in more vocationally focused courses in the Open Tech in the UK, the deep and surface distinction in approach to learning has been identified and found to be a valuable concept for understanding student learning (Strang, 1987). Let's look at how students describe their study in more detail.

We interviewed OU social science foundation course students just after they had completed their study of one block of the course and had submitted the associated assignment (Morgan, Taylor and Gibbs, 1982). We identified the major distinctions of deep and surface approaches to learning, but developed the concepts somewhat so as to describe the complexity of the learning in the OU context. Students' descriptions of note-taking and completing the essay assignment provide useful insights into the learner's world.

Deep approach

As we have already seen, a deep approach to learning is concerned with relating ideas together, finding the main points in a text and constructing meaning from learning material. Also from the research summarized above and also from the examples of understanding in everyday settings, it seems that this process requires the learner to engage in a 'destructuring' of the subject material, followed by a 'restructuring', so this new material is related to the learner's existing understanding. Some students described the process of restructuring in personal terms; they related the material to their own lives and themselves as individuals, for example:

> I read the thing pretty quickly and then go through it again and extract things which seem relevant . . . if I can see that they have an application or are relevant to life as I see it . . . they strike a chord and I take note.

Other students made direct reference to how doing the assignments helped them to clarify their ideas.

> I find the TMAs [tutor-marked assignments] actually crystallize ideas a lot, you know, I read a block and I end up with lots of what are essentially jumbled thoughts, I am not saying they don't make sense but there is no actual structure to them. You can see that one person says this and one person says that . . . How those different ideas relate to each other in my mind comes clear when I start writing about it. I try and construct a pattern I suppose and then fit different authors' ideas into it and agree or disagree depending on the point I am trying to make.

Descriptions of student learning where there is reference to personal involvement seem to parallel Carl Rogers' (1969) concept of 'significant learning'. Learning has a quality of personal involvement, the whole person with his or her feelings as well as cognitive aspects – a feeling of being *in* the learning event.

In contrast to a personally involved approach, some students seemed to be adopting a deep approach, but in a rather external, impersonal or purely cognitive manner. This can be interpreted as a 'strategic' approach to study. For example:

> I think on some of the essay questions you have to go a bit deeper and beyond the definitions in the block [the teaching text] and perhaps try and read a bit and become analytical and critical, but this involves time, which is a precious commodity. I tend to concentrate on the middle course of getting what's in the block.

This type of approach can be successful in terms of the assessment requirements, but students seem to realize that learning could be a more personally rewarding activity in other contexts.

The same student's description of note-taking suggested a deep approach, but using the fastest, most strategic method, as follows:

> I have a quick look and see how long I am going to take on it then I just read straight through it and use the felt tip pen . . . I ring various theories as I go through it and I make a few notes on small index cards on what the various theories are . . . What I tend to put down are the main points in each block. To be quite fair about the way I am doing it I suppose I am doing the minimum study to sort of achieve the end result and so from that point of view, my need is to have something which is more succinctly encapsulated and I use the [index] cards in that fashion.

If we return briefly to the idea of conception of learning, discussed in Chapter 3, we can see a parallel to the distinction between Säljö's levels 4 and 5. Level 4 is concerned with the abstraction of meaning, but in a purely cognitive fashion, in the way the student above is attempting to learn the 'main points' from the correspondence text, but by a minimalist strategic approach.

Surface approach

Students who adopt a surface approach to learning are concerned with memorizing details, with the emphasis on assimilation of knowledge and information and an external emphasis on assessment tasks. Our interviews with OU students revealed the characteristics of a surface approach, and also some variations within a surface approach. Rather than seeing a surface approach as lacking any reflection in learning, we identified students who were attempting different ways of studying, but still directed at the same goal, ie to reproduce information. The ways in which students described their note-taking provide powerful insights into how students tackle their studies. For example:

I have been writing what I consider to be quite a lot of notes. This time the only notes I have really taken are to do with the written assignment. I have taken some notes on that, but the rest I have been putting on audiotape, which I am trying to learn . . . I think it comes over better, you know, getting it on an oral basis rather than reading it all the way through because a lot of these notes were just a matter of sheer copying from the unit [the correspondence teaching text]. In the first three blocks I got a fail in each of them, I wrote dozens and dozens of pages of notes . . . I don't know quite how to explain it. You start something and you think you've got to learn all that lot. But on the tape it doesn't seem to be so much.

This student seems to perceive learning as memorization and is attempting to record information on audiotape as a way to reproduce the material, after having difficulty taking notes. Although different methods of learning have been attempted, the student appears to be constrained in a surface approach to learning, as a consequence of a particular conception of learning.

In contrast to the example above, where there was some attempt at 'variation' within a surface approach, we found other students who were unclear of the demands of academic study in the OU and had difficulty coping with the large amounts of information transmitted by the university. For example:

I just think I harped back to school days too much and I am surprised that there aren't the facts there presented for me . . . I don't know . . . But I do find that with some of the course text, I read it through and I think, oh I don't know what on earth I have read there, I read it through page after page . . . I know I read fast, but I was reading extra slowly to try and take it in. I just wonder if I've got out of the habit of reading and taking things in. Because I read a tremendous amount . . . It is for entertainment more than anything and I tend to skim I suppose . . . But I can't slow my reading down and [this is] coupled with the total inability to make notes.

This student seems to be totally engrossed with himself and with a fear of failure and with apprehension about his ability to study. His attempts to engage with the subject material seem to be of little value, as his apprehension and lack of confidence prevent his study methods from being attempted seriously and evaluated. Also it seems clear that this student perceives learning as 'reproducing information' and consequently is having great difficulty with his studies.

Another variation within a surface approach we identified was how a learner can focus on the fine detail in the correspondence text. This attention to detail, or the 'sign', was in whether the text presented ideas which agreed with or challenged the student's existing understanding and beliefs. This attention to the detail in the text was in terms of right or wrong; this can be interpreted as linked to the student's holding an absolutist conception of learning. This attention to detail has similarities to how Marton and Säljö (1979) described 'horizontalization' – the learner focuses attention on the text all at the same level and fails to grasp its underlying structures. Although the text which a learner is tackling consists of broad principles and specific details, it is seen at one level of information to be evaluated as either right or wrong. This is in contrast to a 'vertical' perception of the text, where the student sees the structure of an argument and can differentiate between specific details and broader principles and theories.

Again we can see that students who are adopting surface approaches to their studies are constrained by their conceptions of learning. Surface approaches to learning all seem to be linked to Säljö's conceptions 1, 2 and 3 (described in Chapter 3) where learning is perceived as a relatively passive acquisition of knowledge without transformation by the learner.

The close relationship between conception of learning and approaches to learning has also been demonstrated empirically by van Rossum and Schenk (1984).

How does approach to learning relate to more vocationally focused education and training courses? Are the variations in approach to learning relevant? From the discussion at the start of this Chapter and also in Chapter 3, I have argued that gaining a full understanding of some phenomenon, concept or set of procedures requires a 'restructuring' of the material in question by the learner. Also in the debates about knowledge and competence, the position set out in Chapter 3 stressed the importance of 'understanding' as the underpinning of 'competence'.

If we return to the work of Strang (1987) with open learning students in the Open Tech (in the UK) engaged in technician education in general engineering subjects, we see the relevance of approach to learning. She used the framework of approaches to learning and conceptions of learning as a basis for understanding 'hidden barriers' to learning experienced by Open Tech students. As Strang explained (1987, pp 36–7)

> Derek's motivation was mainly [vocational intrinsic], he wanted to equip himself to do a job at work. He wasn't bothered about qualifications and there appeared to be no external pressure on him. In addition there was a strong element of personal involvement and the desire to enhance his independence by developing new learning skills.
>
> Yet Derek was not a very successful learner . . . He was asked about his approaches to learning, and some examples give clues as to why he was not successful: 'I try to remember as much as I can to start

off with . . .'; 'electrics are a black art to me . . .'; 'what I'm hoping to do is go over it and if I can remember something different each time . . .'; 'if I don't understand something more or less straightaway then the best thing is just to carry on . . .'; 'I do concentrate, it just doesn't always register . . . I don't know why . . . chromosomes or something like that.'

Clearly Derek lacks confidence in his studies. Whether this is linked to previous unsuccessful attempts at study or perhaps some sort of emotional barrier to getting to grips with 'the black art of electrics', it is not possible to tell without more data. However, the way he described his attempts at study are consistent with a surface approach to learning; he was trying to memorize as much of the material as possible by going through it repeatedly. Although we do not know the background of the course, its pedagogy and assessment, etc, in detail, it seems clear that this student's approach to study is a barrier to understanding and engaging with the teaching and learning materials. So in terms of improving students' learning, to engage with them to help develop their conceptions of learning and their approaches to study are some of the 'interventions' which are available to us as teachers, trainers and course designers.

Helping students to take a deep approach

As teachers, trainers and course designers, how can we help students with their approach to learning? More specifically what can we do which will encourage and facilitate students to take a deep approach to learning? These questions are particularly important in open and distance learning when the facility for interaction with our students is severely limited due to factors of space and time. In Chapter 3 we saw how developing students' conceptions of learning is one of the key areas in which we can help students to develop as learners. The other key area is course design and assessment. How students cope with the assessment system is discussed in Chapter 5. In this section, I shall look briefly at what we can do as course designers and trainers to encourage students to engage actively with the learning materials.

Course design and approaches to learning

In open learning and distance education, text is likely to be the predominant medium for teaching and learning, so I shall concentrate on this area. The essential question for all teachers and course designers is how can we best structure our teaching texts to encourage students to engage actively with the materials and take a deep approach to learning? There is a vast literature on various attempts which have been made to encourage students to engage actively with learning texts. In fact one of the central concerns of educational technology has been how best to structure textual materials so as to facilitate learning (see eg, Rowntree, 1982). Although much of the work of course designers and educational technologists is concerned with encouraging and facilitating students to adopt a deep approach to their learning, detailed understanding of students' experiences of such learning materials is often lacking.

Activities in text

Much of the work to include self-assessment questions and other activities in text has to a large extent been taken on trust. Although the theoretical groundings for the use of inserted in-text questions are rarely discussed explicitly, the origins are derived from programmed learning and mechanistic models derived from behavioural psychology. The assumption is that it is possible to manipulate how students study with instructional devices and to influence their study behaviours. However, the research evidence which would inform this approach to instructional practice is derived from experimental studies in controlled settings, hence extrapolation to the students engaged in their normal settings is extremely difficult (Rickards and Denner, 1978).

Studies on the influence of activities in text carried out by Ference Marton and the Gothenburg Group provide interesting insights into student learning (Marton and Säljö,1984; Dahlgren, 1975). Studies have been carried out to look at how students' approaches to learning can be modified by the use of inserted in-text questions. More particularly, can activities in text encourage students to take a deep approach to learning? These research studies were conducted in 'loosely controlled' settings with valid learning tasks, complete textbook chapters, instructions for the learners to scan or review the text in whatever way they wished, with the aim being to simulate the normal learning environment as closely as possible. The conclusions from this research are that rather than the in-text questions helping students to a deep approach to learning, the opposite occurred. Students working on text which incorporated in-text questions were induced into taking a surface approach to learning in these research studies. It seems that the presence of such questions can 'interrupt' the learners' 'flow' of interaction and engagement with the text. Marton and Säljö explained these results in the following way:

How can this rather clear difference in performance be accounted for? The explanation, in our view, reveals a fundamental aspect of how students adapt themselves to the demands they are exposed to. What happened was that the participants invented a way of answering the interspersed questions *without* engaging in the kind of learning that is characteristic of a deep approach. The technique they used was simply to read the text in such a way that they were able to *mention* . . . the contents of the various parts of each section in a rather superficial way. Thus the task is transformed into a rather trivial and mechanistic kind of learning, lacking the reflective elements found to signify a deep approach. (Marton and Säljö, 1984, p 48)

Of course, these findings could have arisen from the nature of the studies and the quality of the in-text questions. However, for informing our practice, these studies raise serious doubts about attempts to manipulate learners towards a deep approach to learning.

So in terms of course design in open and distance learning, the research does not really give clear guidelines to inform practice. However, it does suggest how relatively easily students can be induced into adopting a surface approach to learning. In contrast, for students to engage actively with textual materials and take a deep approach to learning, they need to become more reflective about their own efforts at studying and understanding.

The research by Lockwood (1992) with OU students engaged in their normal studies gives valuable insights into students' experiences of activities in OU texts. By using individual interviews and open-ended questionnaires Lockwood described students' responses to activities under three main headings of 'course focused', 'self focused' and 'assignment focused'. Students chose to work on activities depending on how they perceived the relevance of them to their own interests and purposes in studying. They operated what was termed a 'cost-benefit' analysis in relation to activities in the text. Students were then conscious actors in the study process, in contrast to being manipulated and controlled by instructional devices, in the way that traditional educational technology and programmed learning tends to assume.

If we look at course design in a way which recognizes learners' conscious control over what they do and how they do it, we can see a rather different pattern emerging for informing practice in the design of learning materials. For example, Rowntree (1992) has developed the notion of the 'Reflective Action Guide' as a progression from the idea of the tutorial-in-print, which has informed much of the use of activities and self-assesment questions in self-instructional teaching texts. For Rowntree (1982) the tutorial-in-print and the use of activities in text have probably been the 'bread and butter' of designing learning materials in open and distance learning. These ideas have also had wide influence at the international level in distance education. Keegan (1986), in his discussion of interaction and communication in distance education, makes many references to self-assessment questions, exercises and self-check tests as key features of the communication system in distance education. If we look at the way self-assessment questions and activities in-text have been used in recent years in open and distance learning, I think much of the approach has been a pragmatic one. This approach entails retaining some of the features of activities, which originated in programmed learning, but attempting to use them practically as devices which logically should help students to learn, in the sense of 'learning by doing'. Perhaps this could be termed a sort of 'neo-programmed learning'. To go further, it could be suggested that they have become the orthodox practice, which is adopted and replicated uncritically. The research of Lockwood (1992) suggests that in spite of these efforts at the pragmatic level, students cannot be easily manipulated by activities in text. This work helps us to look at practice in open and distance learning through a new lens.

If we return to the notion of the 'Reflective Action Guide' (Rowntree, 1992), we can see that there is a clear role to draw the learner more responsibly into the process. There may be activities in the text, but they are open-ended and learners are invited to relate the teaching material they are engaged with to their own personal contexts. The overall framework for learning is set out by the teacher or trainer, but the precise outcomes will be influenced by the learner. The implicit assumptions about how students learn are located more clearly within constructivist theories of learning.

Dialogue in open and distance learning

Writing on distance education, Evans and Nation (1989a) argue that the concept of 'dialogue' should be placed at the centre of the teaching-learning process. They provide a convincing critique of distance education and describe how the predominance of the 'teaching package', with its origins in programmed learning, leads to a mass distance education; this has been labelled 'instructional industrialism', with a complex division of knowledge production and distribution. Dialogue is seen as the essential ingredient for ensuring that students engage actively with learning materials. It is the channel of 'human agency' (Giddens, 1984) in relation to other structures within educational institutions.

> We use the term [dialogue] as a general descriptor of the communications which take place between teachers and learners in the field. However we load the term with meanings for our own purposes: *dialogue involves*

the idea that humans in communication are engaged actively in the making and exchange of meanings, it is *not* merely about the *transmission of* messages. We are concerned, above all, to refute approaches to distance education which begin and end with 'technical solutions' to the problems relating to teacher-student interaction.' (Evans and Nation, 1989a, p 37)

The criticisms of Evans and Nation are directed at features of open and distance learning which can be traced to origins in behaviourist psychology and programmed learning. Dialogue can be introduced into a text through the use of multiple voices, which can be 'constructed' or may be with a colleague in the same field discussing key areas of course material. The aim is to go beyond the idea of the teaching text as an authoritative monologue. For example, Nation (1991) explains how he teaches an introductory sociology course with a selection of set books and then a collection of text and audiotape, to draw students into a dialogue to help them to interrogate the set books. Also the style of the assessment is more student-orientated in that it requires them to do assignments which could be described under the label of mini-projects. To develop the facility for dialogue requires a philosophy which recognizes the responsibility and autonomy of the student in the learning process. This will provide a more holistic focus on the experiences of the learner and how aspects of a teaching system can foster or inhibit such autonomy. Evans and Nation (1989a, p 39) set out their views for practice as follows:

> It is essential to recognize that the key to the successful enactment of dialogue in distance education rests not with matters of technique over assessment, course design and delivery, or on media technology selection, but rather it rests on the philosophy of distance education which informs decisions about techniques and technology. We are advocating a philosophy which recognizes students' autonomy and strives for dialogue. It is most important that students are understood as the key agents in their own learning and that both individually and collectively they can (and often do in spite of their closed course materials) shape their own learning, not just in the ways they learn, but also what they learn. Thus dialogue should be encouraged not just between teacher and students, but also between students themselves (study groups, tutorial groups, self-help networks etc) and between them and those in the social contexts within which they live and work. In this respect, dialogue should be encouraged through the course materials by providing the students with knowledge, skills, ideas and values which are relevant to their needs and interests, and which they can use actively to understand, manage and change their social worlds through dialogue with their fellows.

It is interesting here how the concept of dialogue is closely linked to participation in society and the ideas about students managing and changing their social worlds. There seem to be many parallels here to Freire's work (1972) on the dialogical nature of education, which is also located within an analysis of economic and political structures in society.

So in terms of improving learning materials for our students, they need to be developed within a framework which acknowledges their responsibility and autonomy, and at the same time enables them to engage with the various discourses within subject areas. We have seen how technical devices in text can easily induce students to adopt a surface approach to their studies. As we analyse the particular system of open and distance learning in which we are operating, we need to take account of all aspects of the institution which interact with the learner. Again mechanistic models of learning have had considerable influence in open and distance learning, associated with attempts at technical solutions to encourage student engagement with learning materials. However, such attempts at controlling the learner are likely to lead to learners feeling alienated from the organization in contrast to feeling 'connected' (Student Research Centre, 1986).

Harris and Holmes (1976) are also critical of the explicit pedagogy in many OU teaching texts and particularly of the influence of traditional educational technology.

> Our point is that many course team academics have resisted the obvious devices employed by the rational curriculum planners, and have managed to include in their courses materials and arguments which are not intended to be authoritarian didactic pieces of expert knowledge. Some academics do intend their students to seek personal meanings in the texts, to begin to apply the arguments to their own surroundings and so on. However, given the immovable nature of the one-way at a distance teaching system, and the strong possibility of the 'hidden curriculum' fostered by the assessment system, such liberating intentions seem unlikely to be realised. The reality of the OU teaching system for students is one where large quantities of printed material arrive which express necessarily abstract and universalised arguments. No dialogue with the writers can be held concerning the personal relevance of these arguments.

Harris (1987), in his later analyses of the OU, does acknowledge there is more scope for dialogue through local tutorials and residential schools. Also his analysis of the OU was before there was any substantial use of project-based learning (Morgan, 1983). However, I think the insights of Harris from critical theory are valuable as they provide another perspective on the likely experience of students. As teachers and trainers, perhaps our over-zealous efforts to structure our courses and teaching materials can leave students without any feeling of voice or power in the teaching and learning event. This sentiment is expressed by Jeffcoate (1981) in asking, 'Why can't an OU course unit be more like a book?' He makes a useful point that the quality of the interaction with a text depends primarily on how well it is written, rather than on how many teaching devices are included in it.

Although the discussion above has been based on OU teaching texts, the issues are of general concern in open and distance learning, where teaching through text in some form or other is still the predominant medium.

Finally, before we leave the theme of dialogue in this section, I want to draw attention to a very important dimension of course design from the student's perspective, namely student workload. As teachers and course designers, it is fine for us to have grand ideas about student interaction with learning materials, but if the demands of study time are unrealistically high, students will skim the surface of them and end up making somewhat arbitrary guesses about where and how to allocate their time. To put this more formally, excessive workload demands are likely to induce a surface approach to learning. Chambers (1992) provides a useful method for estimating student workload in the context of study in the OU, but it seems widely applicable to open and distance learning. One of the key features in these estimations is that realistic study times are adopted, between 100 words per minute to as low as 40 words per minute for difficult material. These may sound very slow, but these study times include time for reviewing, re-reading and taking a few notes. However, Chambers argues that without a realistic time allocation, students will not be able to engage with the academic discourses in the text, they will skim the surface as they are constantly driven by the demands of various learning tasks and the assessment system.

Conclusion

In this chapter, we have examined the ways that students go about their studies, and particularly the distinction between a deep and surface approach to learning. These concepts have been used to analyse student learning in a range of contexts of education and training. For improving student learning we need to encourage them to adopt a deep approach to learning. On one hand we need to develop students' conceptions of learning, as we saw in Chapter 3. At the same time, as teachers and trainers, we must look carefully at our course designs. Some of the more 'technical' interventions with devices in instructional texts tend not to be successful in the ways we expect. In fact it appears to be very easy to induce a surface approach to learning.

Also we need to take serious account of student workload. Or to put it very simply, for many curricula and courses, if we want our students to really understand the materials, we should reduce the amount we teach them.

Also in terms of our overall course design and our philosophy of open and distance learning, if we start to engage learners in the process of learning, through dialogue, through giving them some degree of responsibility for their learning, through project work, through extended essays or problem-solving activities – essentially the creative use of the assessment system – we are most likely to facilitate them in adopting a deep approach to learning.

How do the issues raised in this Chapter relate to your own education and training and your own learners? Have you ever done any workload estimations of what your own students are expected to do? What are your own 'explanations' for the disappointing performance of some of your students? To what extent can your individual efforts, informed by an understanding of the learner's perspective, help students to take a deep approach to their studies? On the other hand, what are the organizational and structural constraints within your education and training context, which hinder changes in pedagogy?

Chapter 5

What are students supposed to learn?

Introduction

How do students find out what is required of them in a course of study, either in conventional full-time university level education or in open and distance learning? How do they find their way around what often appears to be a new, perhaps almost alien learning environment? As teachers, trainers and course designers how do we communicate our educational aims and objectives to our students? What cues do we offer to help them develop their awareness of the sort of learning we are attempting to encourage? Also, are we convinced that the details of our teaching and learning activities match what we believe to be the aims of our education and training courses? These are the key questions for this chapter. Again the basic premise is that we can learn a vast amount by listening to and attempting to understand students' experiences of learning. Throughout this book I have stressed that this is an essential aspect of being a 'reflective practitioner' in improving student learning.

A recent report from the Council for National Academic Awards (CNAA) is particularly relevant in examining aims of education. The CNAA described a degree-level programme of study as follows:

> the development of students' intellectual and imaginative powers; their understanding and judgement; their problem-solving skills; their ability to communicate; their ability to see relationships within what they have learned and to perceive their field of study in a broader perspective. The programme of study must stimulate an enquiring, analytical and creative approach, encouraging independent judgement and critical self-awareness. (quoted in Gibbs, 1992, p 1)

This statement may appear unexceptional and to be making very obvious points, generally agreed upon throughout higher education. However, if we look at the details of what actually goes on in much of higher education, we can often see a very different picture. Many students perceive the assessment system as making demands upon them which are almost a direct contradiction of the above statement from the CNAA. Also the quality of education in the university and polytechnic sectors has begun to be scrutinized more closely. For example, a recent report from the HMI (Her Majesty's Inspectorate) in the UK on 'The English Polytechnics' provides strong evidence that much of the teaching and assessment is due for urgent critical review, as follows:

> . . . an over-dependence on one-way teaching and learning – often the formal lecture – so that students do not develop a range of skills appropriate to higher education.

> . . . spoon-feeding in lectures, seminars and practical work, so that students become over-dependent on the information selected and provided for them by their teachers.

> . . . assessment methods which place too high a premium on the ability to recall factual information. (HMI, 1990)

Let's pause for a moment over these statements. It may be easy and convenient to dismiss condemning remarks of this type on the grounds that, 'well, it's not like that round here', 'what do you expect in the polytechnics', 'we use a course team approach so our teaching and assessment is commented on by a group of academics', 'we have industrial advisers on our Boards of Study to ensure vocational relevance', 'the Inspectorate don't know what they are talking about', etc, etc – a whole series of rationales for ignoring this type of report. Whether we like it or not, it seems clear that during the 1990s and beyond, the quality of teaching and learning is increasingly likely to be looked at in detail by the governmental and funding agencies. Also although the student body in universities and colleges is relatively conservative, compared to the heady days of the 1960s, student representatives are aware of the potential power, through collective student action, which could be used to exert an influence on teaching and learning methods. Reports such as the one quoted above provide an opportunity to reflect critically on our practice – to ask fundamental questions about what we teach and how we teach it.

In this Chapter, as well as looking at students' experiences of study and how they come to find out what they are supposed to learn, we shall start to look at how *change* in teaching and learning can occur. What are the barriers to changing the assessment procedures? How does the course development process operate in practice? What sorts of teaching and learning activities are most likely to encourage students to take a deep approach to study, with the corresponding improvement of quality in the learning outcomes? (As we saw in Chapter 4, helping students to take a deep approach to learning is one of the fundamental issues for improving learning in education and training.)

Critical reflection on assessment and teaching

If we use the statements from the CNAA and the HMI, above, as starting points, why is there predominance of one-way teaching and learning? What are the barriers to change, to reducing the emphasis on formal lectures? In open and distance learning, questions of this nature seem to be even more pressing. In distance education, the structure of the teaching and learning system, with a much greater separation of the teacher and learner, tends to favour transmission modes of teaching, through the specially prepared correspondence text. What are the organizational constraints and barriers in open and distance learning to producing different forms of teaching which use a range of media in very different ways, so as to encourage student interaction and engagement with the material? The most important step that can be taken to improve student learning is to place existing practices in teaching and assessment under scrutiny. It is so often the 'untheorized practice', teaching and assessing in ways which have become the unquestioned norm for the organization or department, which leads to unfavourable reviews from the Inspectorate, as quoted above.

In this section, I want to return to the approach of 'critical reflection', as a way of looking at our teaching and learning practice. If we look at the experiences of the actors, the students and the teachers, on one hand and the interactions with the organizational structures, on the other, we shall be in a better position to theorize our practice, as the basis for change.

Evans and Nation have introduced the approach of critical reflection in distance education; they explain it as follows:

> Critical reflection is the process through which human beings use their analytical powers to assess elements of their own lives against their explanatory frameworks (theories) . . . Critical reflection requires that social life be understood as problematic. (1989b, p 10)

The purpose of critical reflection in distance education is to extend the more pragmatic approach of Schon (1983, 1987) to include issues concerned with power and structure both at an organizational level and in society at large.

For further discussion of critical reflection, see Kemmis (1985), Carr and Kemmis (1986) and Evans (1991).

Let us return to the comment from the HMI, 'spoon-feeding in lectures, seminars and practical work, so that students become over-dependent on the information selected and provided by their teachers' and 'assessment methods which place too high a premium on the ability to recall factual information.' In conventional universities and polytechnics the formal lecture is the most common way to transmit new information to students. This is not to say that there are not some very good lecturers who provide students with a unique experience of the discourse of a subject area, but rather that the predominance of lectures may not be the best way to structure a course as a whole. If we look closely at how and why there is a predominance of lectures, we would probably find a complex social history of the pedagogy of the institution, which has remained unquestioned and unchallenged for many years. Similarly with the assessment methods, if we look beneath the surface, we will probably find a complex collection of issues which have shaped policy and practice over a long period of time.

Returning again to the report from the HMI, how would this 'translate' into a statement about open and distance learning? There would probably be reference to the structured correspondence text, as high quality didactic teaching material, but with a risk that the somewhat 'explicit' pedagogy in many courses can lead students to 'reproducing' strategies in their study, unless there are creative and challenging uses of the assessment system. The criticism of the explicit pedagogy in the OU due to the influence of rational curriculum planning and instructional technology has been made by Dave Harris (see Harris and Holmes, 1976, and Harris, 1987).

In the OU, where the correspondence text forms the predominant teaching method, coupled with the complex division of labour involved in knowledge production and distribution, this creates an educational organization which has been labelled 'instructional industrialism' (Evans and Nation, 1989b). There are parallels between the Fordist models of industrial production (mass-production assembly line organization, with a complex division of labour and task specificity) and knowledge production and distribution in mass distance education systems (Campion, 1990; Farnes, 1993). Although considerable effort goes into the preparation of self-instructional texts with the structuring of activities to encourage student engagement with the text (Lockwood, 1992), the taken-for-granted nature of what a course consists of can obscure detailed discussion of potential alternative approaches to course design.

In many open and distance learning systems, residential schools form an essential part of the teaching and learning, often being a mandatory course requirement. So attendance at residential school (combined with a 'reasonable amount' of work) can be seen as part of the assessment requirement (although there is no formal grading). Residential schools provide an important contribution to the student experience; they offer a unique opportunity for dialogue with the likely beneficial influence on student learning. Although a residential component can be a very intellectually stimulating part of a distance education course, which helps students to take a deep approach to their studies, this approach to teaching can be adopted without a thorough evaluation of its strengths and weaknesses. Again, this can be seen as another example of 'untheorized practice' (see for example Morgan and Thorpe, 1993). For example, in distance education in Australian universities, in the 'dual-mode' system, where off-campus students studying part-time can follow the same courses as the full-time on-campus students, weekend schools are widely used.

What do we see when we look in more detail at the history of these schools and how students cope with them? In some cases these residential weekend schools originate in early attempts to provide for off-campus students, with a combination of face-to-face teaching in 'accelerated weekend schools', backed up by some self-instructional materials. These weekend schools are stimulating events. However, in many cases students are expected to be in at least two places at once, if they are following more than one course! In terms of organizational development, this type of timetabling problem needs attention across an entire college from directorate level. However, this type of managerial issue poses dilemmas, as of course it is almost impossible to avoid timetable clashes.

How do students cope with this? How do they play the system? The more 'clued-up' students tackle the organizational constraints by collaborative working. They share lecture notes and laboratory reports, and also delegate certain individuals to go to particular lectures on behalf of the group. In an evaluation study I carried out in Australia, I observed this collaborative working in action. It was a very sophisticated way to manage the demands made by residential schools. Unfortunately, the students who did not have a group of peers for this collaborative approach struggled with their courses. The problem of coping with the laboratory components which were mandatory assessment requirements was particularly severe.

Let's look at how these insights into the teaching and learning process were gained. In methodological terms, how was the evaluation carried out? This understanding of the problems of the teaching and learning was gained by seeking to understand the student's perspective. The evaluation was carried out using a combination of observation, interview and questionnaire – essentially an illuminative approach to evaluation (Parlett and Hamilton, 1977).

So we can see that critical reflection on our teaching and assessment practices is a fundamental tenet in this book, and paying particular attention to students' experiences. In this review process, it is the assessment which stands out as a priority area for our attentions. My colleague Derek Rowntree in his excellent book on assessment stated the problem as follows:

> If we wish to discover the truth about an educational system, we must look into its assessment procedures. What student qualities and achievements are actively valued and rewarded by the system? How are its purposes and intentions realised? To what extent are the hopes and ideals, aims and objectives professed by the system ever truly perceived, valued and striven for by those who make their way within it? The answers to such questions are to be found in what the system requires students to *do* in order to survive and prosper. The spirit and style of student assessment defines the *de facto* curriculum. (Rowntree, 1977, p 1)

These observations by Rowntree are particularly pertinent when we start to look at how students perceive the demands made upon them and how they come to negotiate the assessment system. As teachers, trainers and course designers, it may be difficult to entertain the notion of taking account of students' perceptions of assessment (in addition, of course, to awarding them scores for their efforts, or lack of them, as part of our selection procedures). Surely all our assessment is validated by the external examiners, so why do we need to listen to students?

I believe that students can provide unique insights into our teaching, learning and assessment procedures, which from our respective positions as teachers and course designers, almost by definition are very difficult to get. Of course we can make considerable progress in our own reviewing of assessment procedures. However, if we are to take more of an action research approach to improving our teaching and learning, we need to take more serious account of students. After all they are participants in the process of learning. Also, mature students, who tend to predominate in open and distance learning, are unlikely to tolerate arrogance and indifference towards them from teachers and their institutions. If they believe our student assessment is unfair and punitive, they will walk away and choose to study where they believe their efforts and achievements will be judged fairly against criteria which are openly communicated to them.

Consider your own teaching and training for a moment in your own institution. Are there any recent changes in the assessment practices? Has there been any significant change in what is assessed and how it is assessed? Finally, have any attempts been made to draw students into the assessment process, so as to recognize them as responsible adults?

How do students respond to the demands of assessment? If we look at further research which has attempted to understand the student perspective, we gain a depressing picture. It is not uncommon to find that the assessment system has all sorts of 'side-effects'. The notion of side-effects is a parallel to the use of drugs in medical treatment; are the side-effects permissible and are risks worth taking?

The research of Becker, Geer and Hughes (1968) provides important insights into teaching and assessment. Their book, *Making the Grade – The Academic Side of College Life* is a classic work on the side-effects of assessment. In this work, the research team spent two years living and working in the University of Kansas, observing classes, interviewing students and teachers. They found that grades were generally regarded as the prime focus of everyone's attention. The 'grade-point-average' (to use the American terminology) had become the 'campus currency' – grades were the commodity which were most commonly valued by the institution. Although some students considered scholarship and personal growth to be valuable aspects of the university experience, this was not shared by everyone. In contrast, the value of grades was recognized by everybody.

Some students were clearly aware that what was demanded by the assessment was in direct conflict with scholarship and real understanding. Success in the institution's terms – scores on tests, etc – could be achieved without understanding. A student interview makes this point powerfully:

> There's an awful lot of work being done up here for the wrong reason. I don't exactly know how to put it, but people are going through here and not learning anything at all . . . There's a terrific pressure on everybody here to get good grades . . . There are a lot of courses where you can learn what's necessary to get the grade and when you come out of the class you don't know anything at all. You haven't learned a damn thing, really. – In fact, if you try to really learn something, it would handicap you as far as getting a grade goes. (Becker, Geer and Hughes, 1968, p 59)

The conflict between getting the grade and 'really learning something' can be seen as an unintended side-effect of the assessment system. The pervasive influence of assessment defined the institutional context for studying. The grade-point average became the 'campus currency'.

New students need to establish what type of focus on grades is demanded by the institution or by a particular course. This applies equally to all levels of education and training. This may well be in conflict with students' expectations of a particular course and the espoused aims of the college. We have seen in Chapter 2, in the section 'Why Study?', that students' main aims, attitudes and values in undertaking study vary widely and sometimes result in a mismatch with the demands and requirements of the institution. If we are to help students and take improving student learning seriously, we need to communicate our assessment demands clearly. Also what is the scope for students to negotiate some of the details of what they prepare and submit for assessment? With mature adult learners, to allow them some degree of freedom to negotiate their studies would seem appropriate to acknowledge their previous learning from experience. Although this learning may not be formal academic learning, it is likely to be a significant dimension in students' aims and aspirations in their present study. In Chapter 3 we saw some of the attempts to implement the 'assessment of prior learning' as part of the work to judge 'competence' in the National Vocational Qualifications.

If we return to the report on polytechnics at the beginning of this chapter, the assessment procedures are clearly identified as problematic – 'placing too high a premium on the ability to recall factual information'. Although this report was prepared almost twenty years after the research of Becker, Geer and Hughes (1968), many of the dismal activities which students are required to do, merely reproducing information that's necessary to get the grade without really understanding very much, seem to continue unchanged. In Chapter 4 we saw that the same problem is still identified in current research in student learning; there is a mismatch between the requirements of the assessment and enhancing the quality of student learning.

The organizational context and the learning milieu

The concept of the 'learning milieu' is important for understanding the organizational perspective on teaching and learning. It helps us to address questions about *changing* our educational practices and what sorts of barriers to change exist. As soon as we contemplate changes in the student assessment system, we come up against a complex network of histories, traditions and curriculum practices. The organization itself has a 'dynamic conservatism' (Schon, 1973) in the sense that many of the norms, values and ideologies are reproduced and transmitted within the organization, almost irrespective of the individual members of staff working there. An understanding of the 'organizational milieu' is essential, both in conventional educational settings and in open and distance learning, if we are going to be in a position to implement *change* in our practices.

Improving our students' learning involves critical reflection on the spirit and style of our assessment procedures. I shall quote from case study research into course development in distance education at an Australian dual-mode university (Altrichter, Evans and Morgan, 1991). Although much of the literature on curriculum development and educational technology discusses a rational systems approach to course development (see for example, Rowntree, 1982), there are other important organizational factors.

> Course development does not occur in a neutral, consensus 'vacuum', devoid of actors – on the contrary, it occurs in a complex organizational setting with a culture and a history, both of which have a crucial influence on the course development and production process. (Altrichter, Evans and Morgan, 1991, p 23)

In this case-study research the aim was to understand how a novel course, in terms of its content, pedagogy and assessment, came to be produced. The aim was to understand the course development process so as to take account of the interactions of structures and human agency. The research perspective adopted was similar to that of Meek.

> The task is to enquire into what Giddens (1976, p 161) calls the 'duality of structure', that is 'to explain how it comes about that structures are constituted through action, and reciprocally how action is constituted structurally.' An analysis of the complex interplay between human action and social structure is impossible without the use of the historical perspective. The structure of the situation in which people participate, for example, is neither static nor given in a ready made fashion. Structure, on one hand arises from particular historical circumstances, and on the other, is a force for conflict and change. (Meek, 1983, p 3)

I have quoted from this research, as this methodological basis seems pertinent to debates about assessment and, more important, about how we change our practice.

I hope I can raise your awareness about the crucial teaching and learning issues in your own organizational settings, by drawing attention to students' experiences of assessment. Also, as we look at organizational change, a complex web of social histories is drawn into the foreground. Although these examples refer to higher education, it is possible to see links and parallels to education and training in a wide range of settings.

I want to look now at more of the detail of the learning milieu, which is clearly a key dimension of the overall organizational milieu. The learning milieu will have a major influence on students' experiences, both in terms of teaching methods and assessment.

Departmental styles

The style of departments has a big impact on the experience of being a student. Of course, this is likely to be most significant in face-to-face educational conventional settings. However, with the growth of self-instructional materials in many universities and polytechnics to complement formal lectures and tutorials, these departmental styles are very relevant to the concerns of this book. Also, for open and distance learning courses developed in the industrial and vocational sector, there are styles and traditions, both within the industry and in the professional bodies, which may be involved in course accreditation.

The popular image of the 'university' is that of an organization committed to learning, research and scholarship. These aims of the university (or any institution of higher education) are set out in prospectuses. These documents constitute part of the 'official curriculum', the public face or the espoused aims of the organization. Similar messages may also be transmitted, for example, in a Vice-Chancellor's address to new students. This will almost certainly stress how the university experience provides students with a unique opportunity for intellectual and social development. Alas these aspirations of university study are not always realized when new students actually get to their particular faculties or departments.

At the departmental level, there are many variations in how these espoused aims are translated into what students are going to experience in physics, biology, anthropology, or whatever. Examining a number of introductory departmental addresses shows striking differences, not only in what actually occurred, but more important, in the implicit messages they transmitted to students as to what was going to be required of them, in terms of the teaching and assessment. Staff often express their likely demands in very different terms. Their introductions for new students often convey key messages about the distinctive atmospheres or milieu of different departments. Here are three examples (Parlett, 1977, pp 175–6). In one case, the head of a science department spoke for forty minutes, outlining what would be expected of the students, as follows:

> You will take this – tackle this – you must submit so many laboratory reports.

Half his talk was spent on assessment regulations and the other half on aspects of student failure. There was an elaborate description of how weaker students were not failed early in the course but allowed to continue. The weaker students knew they would have to do better in the next year. As the head explained:

You see it's entirely up to you whether you fail or not.

The overwhelming message was that it was going to be tough and hard work. Some would fail as a penalty for not meeting the regulations. The control of the course content and the assessment procedures lay firmly in the hands of the department. Students were in the department to be subservient to this group of academic scientists. Finally, the role and nature of assessment was made thus:

> Statistically some of you are bound to fail – but you won't fail unless your reports are late, or poor work is submitted – if you work satisfactorily you'll make it. We are looking for about one failure a year – so you can decide for yourselves.
> (Nervous laughter from the students as they look around at each other.)

For a very different style, we can look at a particular arts department. The chairperson of the faculty board gave a brief chatty introduction.

> University will be a time during which you should take a critical look at yourselves and rethink things. It should be interesting, stimulating – intellectually fun.

He stressed how students should keep in contact with their tutors and, of course, problems would crop up, both course related problems and personal problems. However, the emphasis conveyed to students was, 'Do come and talk with us'. The group then broke into smaller tutorial groups to explore particular course options. Information was given on the expected work load and assessment requirements. The discussion then turned to a more informal style about students' reasons for choosing that department. The afternoon finished with a wine and cheese party.

The third example indicates an even more informal approach. This department explicitly set out to establish an informal atmosphere, with a belief that for staff and students to know each other at a personal level was beneficial to teaching and learning. The department's efforts started before formal registration, by taking applicants around the department, meeting both staff and students. Once enrolled, students each had their own academic, social and personal adviser. Early in the course, students went on a residential field trip and this helped staff and students to get to know each other at a personal level, and enabled students to begin to feel they 'belonged' to a department.

Obviously introductory sessions are at a very general level. But they can provide new students with the first cues of what is going to be required of them. These introductions form an integral part of shaping the academic environment. They provide the first signpost for students as to what it is going to be like in college.

As teachers, trainers and course designers in open and distance learning, what do our introductory sessions with students look like? In our initial contact with the students as the tutor or counsellor, what aspects of being students do we emphasize? Is the communication concerned about deadlines for assignments, stressing that they are 'absolute', and that lateness of any sort will not be tolerated? Alternatively, does this communication try to establish the 'human dimension' of study for the distance learner? Research at the OU into aspects of student academic support at the local level suggests that the 'human dimension' to study provided by the local tutor or counsellor is vitally important for many students. The human dimension can serve to create a 'feeling of belonging' to a university, with a sense of 'connectedness', in contrast to the experience of being a distance education student as a feeling of isolation and 'alienation' (Student Research Centre, 1986). In open and distance learning, a complex collection of issues shapes the learning milieu. Establishing a feeling of 'connectedness' is likely to be immensely important for enhancing students' experiences in open and distance learning.

For adult learners studying part-time by open learning, besides details of a course and an educational institution, there are interactions in the workplace and in the domestic setting, which are important aspects of the learning milieu. Students engaged in open learning in the workplace may find that studying raises complex issues with work peers about the nature and purpose of work. The workplace may be thought of by some employees only as a place for manufacturing and production, and attempts by trainees to develop new skills and gain qualifications may be treated with some degree of scorn. In other cases, learning on the job may be the norm in the organization, which provides a supportive learning environment involving staff across different levels. An example from a study of adult learning in the workplace illustrates some of the complexity of the milieu. Chris works as a production supervisor:

> Chris's work milieu is complex: it includes, as well as staff in her unit and the manager, other people who relate to her unit. They all have expectations and presuppositions about the work, the organization, the procedures of her work area and the greater organization within which she works – its values and the way it is perceived within local society. This is the environment within which she is constantly interacting, and which contributes to her experience. Within this context, she has to find opportunities for learning. (Boud and Walker, 1991, p 17)

Although the workplace may be a complex context for engaging in learning, it is very different from the problems of learning in the domestic setting, experienced by some women students. In Chapter 6, we shall see how the gains from OU study can lead to personal change and development. In one case this change created a tension and polarization in a student's relationship with her partner, which resulted in her almost studying 'in secret'.

The learning milieu in fiction

If we step outside an academic analysis for a moment and look to fiction, we find that teaching and assessment appear regularly, both in novels and in the fictional portrayals of academic life. It seems that the humour of Laurie Taylor, in his column in *The Times Higher Education Supplement,* and the writings of David Lodge are so successful because they portray such a 'ring of truth', which mirrors the unspoken realities and shady corners of teaching and learning in universities, colleges and training organizations.

David Lodge in *Changing Places* (1975) portrays Philip Swallow, a Visiting Professor at the plate glass and concrete jungle of Euphoria State University in the USA on the annual academic exchange from the University of Rummidge, a red-brick university in the UK. Professor Swallow is beginning to settle in when he hears about student evaluations of teaching published in the *Course Bulletin*, a sort of consumer guide to the courses and teachers, produced by the students. Professor Swallow has just met Wily Smith, the author of the *Course Bulletin*, who is wearing a badge bearing the words, 'Keep Kroops'.

> Kroops turned out to be the name of an Assistant Professor in the English Department who had recently been refused tenure. 'But there's a grass-roots movement to have him kept on here,' Wily explained. 'Like he's a real groovy teacher and his classes are very popular. The other professors make out he hasn't published enough, but really they're sick as hell because of the raves he gets in the *Course Bulletin*.' – Wily produced the current issue from one of his capacious pockets.
>
> 'You won't be in there, Professor Swallow. But you will next quarter.'
> 'Really?' Philip opened the book at random.
> **English 142. Augustan Pastoral Poetry. Asst. Professor Howard Ringbaum. Juniors and Seniors. Limited enrolment.**
> *Ringbaum, according to most reports, does little to make his subject interesting to students. One commented: 'He seems to know his material very well, but resents questions and discussion as they interrupt his train of thought.' Another comment: 'Dull, dull, dull.' Ringbaum is a strict grader and according to one report likes to set insidious little quizzes.'*

'Well', said Philip with a nervous smile. 'They certainly don't mince their words, do they?' He leafed through other pages on English courses.

English 213. The Death of the Book? Communication and Crisis in Contemporary Culture. Asst. Professor Karl Kroops. Limited enrolment.

Rise early on Enrolment Day to sign on for this justly popular interdisciplinary multi-media head-trip. 'Makes McLuhan seem slow,' was one comment, and another raved: 'the most exciting course I have ever taken.' Heavy reading assignments, but flexible assessment system. Kroops takes an interest in his students, is always available. (Lodge, 1975, pp 67–8)

As far as it is possible to judge from these student evaluations of teaching, I would much prefer to be enrolling with Professor Kroops, if I were a student! If you were a member of staff lobbying for change in teaching and assessment in your department as a 'new innovator' (with exceptional reviews of your teaching – a Professor Kroops, if you like!), it might not be surprising if the 'old guard', as represented by Professor Ringbaum, would not be supporting your tenure applications.

In terms of the concerns of the present book, David Lodge's student evaluations of teaching highlight important issues for the student's experience, 'the insidious little quizzes', on one hand and 'the flexible assessment system and taking an interest in students', on the other. We can see that the nature of quality in teaching and assessment may well be a highly contested issue, one which can bring all the micro-politics and sub-cultures in academic departments into the foreground. In terms of changing our teaching and assessment procedures, we have to operate in the realities of these organizational milieux.

Finally, before we move away from fiction, if you were writing an entry about your own course for a 'Course Bulletin' (like Wily Smith) what features of the assessment procedures would you want to draw to the attention of your potential students? Also if you were being very honest, what would be the negative features or problems you would refer to?

Try writing your entry for a 'Course Bulletin', role-playing your students if you like. And be honest in what you say! For all you know there may be a 'Wily Smith' out there among your students, preparing a report on your courses for the next 'alternative prospectus' in your college.

The learning milieu and approaches to study

Why have I emphasized the concept of the learning milieu and the styles of academic departments? The nature and atmosphere of the learning environment influences how students tackle their study, ie their approach to study, and (as we saw in Chapter 4) this is closely linked to the quality of the learning outcomes. In Chapter 6 we look at what students gain from study, ie the quality of the learning outcomes.

Researchers have recently become interested in students' perceptions of the learning environment and their approaches to studying. Studies using questionnaires to gain students' views on formality of teaching, the nature of assessment procedures, the workload, etc, have found a link between departments rated highly for 'freedom in teaching and learning' and their students taking a deep approach to study, as rated on the questionnaire (Entwistle and Ramsden, 1983). We have already seen in Chapter 4 the variations in approaches to study and how they have an influence on the learning outcomes, i.e. what is actually learnt.

Here are some examples of the items from these questionnaires:

- How much help is given with study problems?
- How competent and well prepared are the staff?
- How much choice and control do you have over the content and method of studying?
- How friendly are the staff?
- How prepared are they to adapt to students' needs?
- How heavy is the workload to fulfil the requirements of the syllabus and assessment perceived to be?

These are some of the questions used to characterize students' perceptions of their learning environment. This research evaluates departments under a number of headings: good teaching; freedom in learning; openness to students; workload; social climate. It also described subject area differences under the headings of: formality of teaching methods; clarity of goals and standards; and vocational relevance.

The atmosphere and milieu in various departments conveys clues about what sort of learning and studying are going to be required, and also rewarded, in terms of course credits and good grades. As teachers and course designers, what we assess and how we assess it is probably the most important area available to us for 'interventions' in our attempts to improve student learning. The overall aim of this chapter is to demonstrate the significance of assessment, when we examine students' perceptions of it.

Differences between departments or courses can place somewhat conflicting demands on students. For example, when students are following joint degrees, working across subject areas with different traditions, or engaged in interdisciplinary studies. Here is how one student described interdisciplinary project work in an interview:

> Potentially I'm going to get a lot more out of it [the project] than most other courses. Geography is very good, lots of attention to teaching and learning and personal contact, but Economics is very weak in this respect.

> *Interviewer*: Can you explain what you mean by weak?

> 75% of the Stage Two courses are virtually the same as first year, there's no progression – it hasn't been very intellectually demanding, just get the information from books and put it down on paper – if you put your own ideas into it, you seem to do very badly – that's different from Geography. With one exception, in Economics, the majority of staff are against you putting your own ideas into it – or so it seems – it's very upsetting. It's O.K. for some students, but for anybody involved in the subject, it's very frustrating. (Morgan, 1984)

The requirements of the economics assessment system, as seen by this student, seem to call for reproducing information and not incorporating one's own ideas, in contrast to the geography requirements. Assessment demands of the type which seem to be demanded by economics are likely to induce students to take a surface approach to their studies, as we saw in Chapter 4.

Students' experience of the grading game: coping with assessment

In describing different styles in academic departments, inevitably issues of assessment and grading arise. The assessment system is pivotal when we examine how you find out what you are supposed to learn. Assessment – the 'Big A' appears repeatedly when students discuss teaching and learning! From the students' perspective, the assessment defines the de facto curriculum.

By the time the student quoted above, working for a joint degree in economics and geography, reached her final year, she was very aware of the different demands of the teaching and assessment in the two subject areas. Her work was tailored accordingly for the requirements of the economics assessment system, as she explained:

> If you put your own ideas in, you seem to do badly, so I have stopped doing that now.

It would appear that studying and learning for economics was merely reproducing information from text books and lectures, learning was constrained
by the demands of the assessment system. For many students, writing essays
and then attempting to interpret the sort of grade they get is a powerful way
to 'suss-out' the demands of study, or perhaps the whims of individual members of staff. As one student vividly explained:

> I'd never had less than an A or a B, but here I was with a C on this
> essay. So I went up to see him and asked why . . . and he said: 'Well
> you shouldn't have given me all this stuff about Western countries'
> shortcomings compared with Russia – I've lived there and, believe me,
> you don't know what it's like. What I meant by evaluating the Soviet
> system was for you to concentrate on its own internal problems.' And I
> thought, 'Well why didn't you say that in your essay title, then!' But
> I'll make sure I suss out what his essays are really after next time,
> though, won't I? (Rowntree, 1988, p 148)

Sussing out the assessment system is probably the most important aspect for
students: it is almost a necessary condition for their survival. However, as we
look at the evidence from students in a wide range of educational settings, it
is clear that clarification of the assessment goals would improve the experience of study. This is not to spoon-feed them. No, to the contrary, it is to be
clear and fair about what we expect of our students. Otherwise this communication will only occur through students' efforts at 'cue-seeking' (Miller
and Parlett, 1974).

We have already seen in Chapter 1 (the fictional autobiography), how the
teaching and assessment style in the physics department contributed in some
ways to our student's change of subject and department.

Finding out what you are supposed to learn is linked to the incongruence
between the formal curriculum and what has been termed 'the hidden curriculum' (Snyder, 1971), another way of expressing the conflict between
learning for understanding and learning for examination requirements.
Observations in classrooms at the beginning of term showed that students
were asked to be creative – take intellectual risks. However, some weeks
later students found that the class test required them merely to reproduce a
vast amount of information that could only be mastered by memorization.
There was a huge discrepancy between students' expectations of the course
and what was really required to pass the test. The hidden curriculum, the
required task, was not to be creative or imaginative, rather it was to play a
closely controlled academic game.

As we have already seen in Chapter 4, the demands of assessment which
emphasize memorization will tend to induce students to take surface

approaches to study. Also, many students react to this type of institutional context by withdrawing emotionally. Study can become a cynical ritual focused on fulfilling goals constructed and controlled by an outsider, an alien organization – the college or open learning institute. In a distance learning context the educational institution may be even more remote, leading to feelings of alienation and possibly drop out. We have already seen that an important part of being a student is finding out what you are supposed to learn. Sussing-out the demands of assessment is one of the key 'ingredients' of success for our students.

We have seen how the departmental style contributes to create a particular learning milieu, which implicitly provides cues for what is required. Also the spirit and style of assessment provides a way for students to find out what, from their perspective, is seen to constitute the course.

Some students develop a sophisticated 'cue-consciousness' during the course of their studies (Miller and Parlett, 1974). Besides being aware of the cues formally given by teaching staff as to what is coming up in the examination, other students actively engage in button-holing the staff to probe them for clues about the examination, such as parts of the course which could be omitted, etc. This group of students was described as 'cue-seeking'; they also gained the best results in the final examination. A third group of students was identified. These students were labelled cue-deaf – they assumed that hard work, justice and fairness of the assessment system would stand them in good stead and ensure success.

In the autobiographical account in Chapter 1, our student seemed to be engaged in this type of 'cue-seeking' by jokingly questioning a tutor about the content of the examination. But that was only towards the end of the first year. The first attempts at writing up a laboratory report, early in the first term, seem to display many of the hallmarks of being 'cue-deaf'.

At the more general level, some students appear to go about their work in a focused strategic manner, finding out what is required in assignments before investing study time. This is not to suggest that study is, or should become, some sort of assessment-driven ritual, but for some students it is an activity which becomes the focus of reflection. What's it really about? What do I have to do? Why am I doing this? There are parallels here to the discussion in Chapter 3, 'What Is Learning?', about how learning becomes 'thematized'. The process and activity of learning itself becomes a focus for reflection. Changes of this nature, of seeing aspects of being a student in a different and new perspective are an essential part of developing as a learner.

Looking at dialogue

Dialogue between students and teachers is obviously a most effective medium for students to find out what is required of them in their studies. This process of finding out what you are supposed to do in academic study is vividly portrayed in the film *Educating Rita*, based on the play by Willy Russell (1986).

Rita works as a hairdresser, she comes from a working class background and lives within a traditional family. She left school at the first opportunity with a dislike of school and education. Almost twenty years later, she has enrolled to study the OU Arts foundation course. (The OU operates a system of open access and is often claimed to be the second-chance university for students who were unable to or not interested in continuing their education when 16 or 18 years old. Rita is clearly a student of this type.)

The scene is in the tutor's office, an impressive room with a long history and steeped in academic tradition. Frank is the tutor and also an aspiring poet. Rita is having one of her first tutorials for the course and Frank is returning her first assignment, an essay on Peer Gynt.

Frank:	I want to talk about this that you sent me. (He holds up a sheet of A4 paper.)
Rita:	That? Oh.
Frank:	Yes. In response to the question, 'Suggest how you would resolve the staging difficulties inherent in the production of Ibsen's Peer Gynt, you have written, quote, **'Do it on the radio'**, unquote.
Rita:	Precisely.
Frank:	Well?
Rita:	Well what?
Frank:	Well I know it's probably naive of me but I did think you might let me have a considered essay.
Rita:	That's all I could do in the time. We were dead busy in the shop this week.
Frank:	You write your essays at work?
Rita:	Yeh.
Frank:	Why?
Rita:	Denny gets narked if I work at home. He doesn't like me doin' this. I can't be bothered arguin' with him.
Frank:	But you can't go on producing work as thin as this.
Rita:	Is it wrong?

Frank:	No, it's not wrong, it's just . . .
Rita:	See, I know its short. But I thought it was the right answer.
Frank:	It's the basis for an argument, Rita, but one line is hardly an essay.
Rita:	I know, but I didn't have much time this week, so I sort of, y' know, encapsulated all me ideas in one line.
Frank:	But it's not enough.
Rita:	Why not?
Frank:	It just isn't.
Rita:	But that's bleedin' stupid, cos you say – you say, don't y' – that one line of exquisite poetry says more than a thousand pages of second rate prose.
Frank:	But you're not writing poetry. What I'm trying to make you see is that whoever was marking this would want more than, '**Do it on the radio.**' (Russell, 1986, pp192–3)

I think we can see Rita trying to establish the rules of the game, by submitting her own personal efforts. She subsequently comes to see what is required. She develops as a student and goes on to be a successful and critical and demanding student at summer school.

This is obviously an extreme example from fiction, but, for students in the real world, there are many parallels in how they have to 'suss-out' the system as to what they really have to do to survive. Like Rita, for students in a wide range of education and training, they have to find out the 'rules of the game' of what they are studying.

Dialogue is obviously one of the most effective ways of finding out and facilitating this development as a learner – whether it is with a tutor or with a peer group of students.

Coming back to the example of driving and negotiating the 'funny right turns' in the centre of Melbourne, in Chapter 4, finding out what was needed required me to change my awareness, to see the same information and signposts in a new light, as a new coherent whole. Dialogue and discussion was a key part of this process of change.

Dialogue in distance education and open learning

In distance education or external study, the absence of this opportunity for dialogue, or the much more restricted facility through occasional face-to-face tuition, telephone tuition or correspondence tuition, make this 'finding out' a slower and more difficult process. Many external students stress this feeling of isolation when interviewed about their learning experiences.

> The darkness becomes your closest friend when studying alone – no matter how much assistance is set out – it's difficult to specifically name problems to overcome. Just to have someone there to let you know if you are working on the correct lines.

Clearly for this student, 'setting things out', or telling students what to do did not result in a change of awareness of what to do. The opportunity to discuss the work with a tutor was crucial for the development of confidence in how to tackle the work.

The difficulty of 'telling' students in text-based study guides what is required and actually influencing their study patterns is evident with Open University students. Even after they have completed a number of courses, there can still be uncertainty about the demands of study.

Interviews with students following a third-level education course, where students were given considerable choice as to what materials were studied and in what order, revealed how some of them had failed to appreciate the nature of the course structure (Morgan, 1988). Although the study guides and assessment schedules described where choice was available, these students had not fully understood the demands of the course. A number of factors contribute to this. Some students appeared to have developed a type of 'habitual response' to Open University courses. A majority of courses set out in a fairly high degree of detail what students should learn and how they should go about it. Students who have become accustomed to a sequential study of course materials, followed by an assignment, experience problems with this more flexible structure. For these students, this course requires a change of perception of what constitutes an Open University course, when the university sends out materials in full house-style, which are not intended to be studied at the same depth. These students appear to see all the textual material at the same level and consequently they complain about the high workload.

Other students seemed to have failed to suss-out what was required, partly through lack of time to pay sufficient attention to the introductions and study guides and partly because of their attempts to rush through the printed course material which they assumed constituted the course. As one student explained:

> The assignment I chose needed one section, but I didn't reach it until afterwards . . . with pressure to keep up the reading I didn't concentrate on the essay – this is pointed out – but you tend to slip

back into thinking it's a sequential course – choice is unusual, you don't normally get this amount of it. I didn't realize until summer that you could leave out parts of blocks 3 and 4 – it's a shame really.

Again, with the lack of a campus peer group in distance education, students experienced problems finding out what was required. In spite of guidance 'telling' students what to do, in some cases it was unsuccessful in helping them *change* their awareness of what constituted an Open University course.

Sussing-out what is required in study is a major part of being a student. This seems to apply to education and training in a wide range of settings. In distance education and open learning it can be a difficult and slow process, hence the importance of local tutorial support.

Finding out the demands of new subject areas is a key part of what we might term 'academic socialization', particularly as students move to more specialized courses after broad-based ones at foundation level. As socialization proceeds, so the confidence of the student increases, so that he or she 'knows what is involved' in studying at the Open University and within a particular subject area.

Whether your students are studying in a conventional university or in distance or open learning, the issue of 'academic socialization' is a key part of becoming a student. This aspect of change is looked at in more detail in Chapter 6.

What forms of academic support are most likely to facilitate students' development in their conceptions of learning and in their academic socialization? The activities of writing, trying out ideas, debate and discussion seem most likely to facilitate these developments. All these are aspects of face-to-face tutorial support. The activities play a unique part in helping students to acquire the general insights and competence that foster higher quality learning.

Students realize the importance of tutorials for their development as learners. Although the examples below are taken from distance education, they reflect the usefulness of tutorials for all students. Interviews with students provide many references to how face-to-face tuition is seen as an essential course component which makes a unique contribution to learning. For example:

Interviewer: How do you find tutorials? How would you feel about having fewer tutorials if there were severe financial cutbacks?

Student (studying her 3rd course): That's the worst thing they could do, that would kill it. Where would you go for help if you can't go to your tutorial? You can ring him up, but you

> get more out of discussing in the tutorial – that tutorial is central to everything; it has a social and academic function. They are interlinked – one and a half hours a month is not a lot compared with college – how can you cut down on that? If I hadn't been to that tutorial I wouldn't know what the hell they were talking about. Tutors explain what the course is aiming at – without that tutorial the units would be like a foreign language.

This tutorial function of interpreting the course for students, the tutor, as it were, acting as a cultural mediator, seems to play an essential part in student learning. Dialogue enables students to find out what is required of them in a way which does not occur simply by telling them in study guides or assignment guides, etc, what they should be doing. Students describe tutorials as helping them see the 'wood from the trees' in the course material and how to tackle different subject areas.

As a student taking his first systems course explained:

> I'd missed the tutorial from moving house. I'd not got the necessary base to start on from missing tutorials, so my first two essays, which I thought were the best I'd ever done, got poor marks. I was getting really demoralized. I met my tutor at summer school and sorted it all out and my grades improved. I know what he wanted. I knew what the course wanted – it was a different approach to writing a general type of essay, it was using a systems approach, using diagrams, notes, etc to explain points . . . if I had gone to those early tutorials I would have understood what was wanted.

This function of dialogue seems to play a unique role in helping students construct meaning from course material and at the same time enabling them to grasp what kind of learning is being encouraged by the university. If you are teaching at a conventional polytechnic or university, try to imagine what it would be like for students without any regular tutorial provision or peers to talk to – just lectures and books to learn from. Interpreting the demands of a course is a crucial part of surviving as a student. Coming to understand these demands and being able to cope with them, is the essence of the skilled learner.

As teachers and course designers, facilitating students' development as learners is one of the key challenges for us, in terms of improving practice.

Although the above examples are from distance education, similar issues apply for students engaged in open learning. In the fictional autobiography (Chapter 1), we saw how at the beginning of the first year it is possible to put in a lot of effort but still be very uncertain about its value, in terms of meeting the assessment requirements.

Responding to the institution

So far we have discussed how students come to find out what is required in academic study, as defined by the teacher or institution. However, developing autonomy and independence in learning is an important aim for all education and training. How does developing autonomy and personal responsibility for learning match the teaching and learning provision of an institution?

In chapter 2, under 'Why Study?', we saw the diversity of students' aims, purposes and expectations in studying. The interaction between students' orientations to learning and the course provision of the institution will define how students see themselves. Does a course or faculty tailor teaching and learning activities to meet students' particular interests? Who is in control of the learning – teacher or student? Some institutions are structured around student control of learning. For example, in Europe at the Universities of Bremen, Roskilde and Aalborg, the idea of project orientation forms the entire basis of the curriculum, and in the UK, Independent Studies departments are a way to meet student aims of study (Percy and Ramsden, 1980; Morgan, 1983).

In your own teaching and your own institution, do your students get the opportunity, or are they required, to do project work? As we saw in Chapter 1, projects can be the most rewarding part of an educational programme. In open and distance learning, assignments can be structured so as to allow students some degree of freedom and responsibility in their studies, so as to get them involved in developing a personal significance to their learning, rather than only presenting answers to the questions set by the teachers.

Conclusion

As students develop as learners, they will begin to perceive the demands of their courses through the interactions of departmental style, the nature of the teaching, and the grading and assessment requirements.

As course designers, trainers and teachers we can help students to become more aware of these issues. Structuring facilities for dialogue with a tutor or counsellor in our courses can help students to reflect on learning and to assist their development. This does not imply only face-to-face sessions. Dialogue can be built into written communications, through the creative use of the assessment system. Also, in our course development, we must realize how aspects of teaching and course design, particularly assignments which demand memorization, or at best reproducing information, can easily induce students to take surface approaches to learning. Finally, it is a salutary reminder how often the assessment demands become divorced from requirements of learning and studying for understanding.

Critical reflection on our teaching and assessment practices, so as to recognize the realities of students' experience of learning, will provide a better understanding of how to *change* our practice.

The next chapter will draw together the themes we have discussed so far and set out the issues of 'becoming a student' and how students develop skill in learning. This chapter will also focus on developing a theory of adult change and development, firmly grounded in the learners' realities, and also closely related to improving practice.

Chapter 6

How do students change and develop as learners?

Introduction

This chapter will explore students' experiences of learning in terms of what they actually gain from study. Besides certification of course completion or the award of a qualification, in what ways have students changed and developed as a result of their experience of education and training? What are the knowledge and skills they possess? How has their conceptual understanding changed? How have they developed as learners? How has the experience of study interacted with other dimensions of their lives as adult learners? These are the key questions which are addressed in this chapter. I want to describe change and development in terms of three closely related areas:

(i) The outcomes of learning and conceptual change,
(ii) the development of skill and autonomy in learning, and
(iii) the interactions of study with people's lives.

The outcomes of learning

What do students learn from a course of study? Much of the research on student learning has tended to concentrate on quantitative conceptions of learning and understanding. So scores on tests and examination pass rates tend to be the predominant indicators which are adopted for talking about the success or otherwise of students. Learning is considered in quantitative terms. However, if we look at learning in qualitative terms, we see a rather different picture.

In Chapter 4, we saw how different approaches to learning are directly linked to the quality of the learning outcomes. The arguments presented in Chapters 3 and 4 set out a view of learning which is concerned with a *change* in the way something is understood. This view of learning is in contrast to one which is concerned with the accumulation of information. This section of the Chapter will look at qualitative difference in learning outcomes and also discuss how understanding learning outcomes from the learner's perspective can be used as a basis for improving learning.

The research of Ference Marton and the Gothenburg Group has been very influential in investigating the content of learning (see Marton, Hounsell and Entwistle (1984), Dahlgren, (1984)). Learners have been asked in individual interviews how they understand particular concepts, ideas, theories, etc. The aim is to describe the qualitatively different ways in which individuals experience or conceptualize particular aspects of reality. (This could include the conceptual framework and theories in an open learning text they had been studying, or it could be concerned with aspects of everyday life, of politics or economics, etc). This research is concerned with understanding, analysis and experiential description. Marton (1981) has labelled this field of inquiry as 'phenomenography'. So part of the task in improving learning is to gain a fuller understanding of how learners are attempting to understand learning materials, and what are the various meanings they gain from their studies, for example, from an open learning teaching text, or from studying an article. Research within this tradition has a direct relevance to improving learning, as it gives us insights into students' views of the subject matter. It helps us to understand 'where the student is at' in relation to the subject matter, and find out about beginners' conceptions of the subject. This is not to say that these are 'wrong' as such, but rather that they are relatively unsophisticated conceptions of the subject matter. Qualitative descriptions of learning provide new insights into the quality of learning, and also highlight some of the problems associated with student assessment. I want to explain some of this research and then look at its potential for informing practice in open and distance learning.

Dahlgren and Marton (1978) investigated students' understanding of the concept of 'price' both at the beginning and also at the end of an introductory course in economics, by asking them a question about pricing in an everyday example, as follows: 'Why does a bun cost 50 øre?' (This research was with Swedish students. 100 øre to the Swedish crown.) Students were asked this question in individual interviews, with probing until the interviewer had explored the limits of the subjects' understanding. An analysis of the interview transcripts revealed two fundamentally different ways of explaining 'price'; one referred to the dynamic of the market mechanism influencing price, while the other was 'static' description which implied a value inherent in a particular object. The four categories were explained as follows:

A1 Price is determined by the market conditions, ie supply and demand of its constituents.
A2 Price is determined by the supply and demand for buns.
B1 Price is determined by the sum of the 'value' of its constituent parts.
B2 Price of the bun is equal to its value.

So category A is the dynamic understanding of the concept of 'price' while category B is the static one.

For a group of students just beginning an economics course, it would not be surprising for there to be quite a wide spread across these four different conceptions. However, by the end of an introductory course on economics it would be a reasonable assumption that all the students would have developed their understanding of the subject to be able to give A-type answers to the question. Alas, this was not the case. Although the majority of students passed the examination requirements, many students still held conceptions of 'price' which were analysed as B-type. Students were able to accumulate sufficient marks to gain a pass grade, but their understanding of the basic concepts had not actually developed, certainly as judged by the question about price mechanism, framed in an everyday context. Of course there will always be some 'borderline' students, who scrape through, but, the picture gained from the qualitative description of learning is not very encouraging, when we are concerned to foster quality in student learning. The results of Dahlgren and Marton (1978) draw our attention to some of the key dilemmas in teaching, learning and assessment. How can we engage with the learners' existing conceptions of subject material (in this case static conceptions of price) to enable them to develop to more sophisticated understanding? We shall return to this challenge later.

With OU students we have carried out similar research to look at their conceptual changes as a result of the social science foundation course (Taylor, Gibbs, and Morgan,1981; Beaty, 1987). Students were asked a series of questions, devised by the course team, which were judged to be valid for exploring students' understanding of some of the key concepts taught in one section of the course. Here are three examples of the questions to illustrate the approach to the investigation. To explore the concept of 'capitalism', students were asked, 'Is Britain capitalist?' For the concept of 'division of labour', students were asked, 'In Britain it takes 39 people all doing different jobs to make and sell a pair of sandals. In Morocco it takes one man to make and sell a pair of sandals. Why might this be interesting to social scientists?'

To investigate the concept of 'oligopoly', they were asked, 'Surf, Omo, Radiant are all produced by Lever Bros, while Bold, Tide and Dreft are produced by Procter and Gamble, in fact these two companies produce almost all the soap powder in Britain. Does this matter?'

The questions were framed in everyday language, so that they could be easily understood by students who were just beginning their studies.

We shall look at the interpretations of students' reponses to this last question, about the concept of 'oligopoly' and whether it matters that two companies produce almost all the washing powder in the UK, to demonstrate the insights gained from this type of research. From a detailed reading and rereading of the interview transcripts, the following framework of four qualitatively different ways of responding to the question on oligopoly, in the form of a hierarchy, was derived (Taylor, Gibbs, and Morgan, 1981, pp 11–12).

Conception A The extent to which the price/quality/choice of the product is fixed depends on the *nature* of the cooperation between Lever Bros and Procter and Gamble. This conception is saying that it depends on how closely they were working together. If they do not cooperate at all it would be like free market competition, but if they organize a cartel it would be like a monopoly. So it depends on the nature of any cooperation.

Conception B The price/quality/choice of the product is fixed by cooperation between Lever Bros and Procter and Gamble. In this conception there is no notion of the extent of any cooperation. This B-type conception says essentially that if there are only two producers they will fix the price between them.

Conception C The price/quality/choice of the product is affected by competition or the lack of it. There is no notion of price fixing in this conception. This C-type conception ranges from students who believe that the presence of two companies is the same as having perfect competition to those who believe it is the same as having a monopoly.

Conception D Choice is affected by the advertising and marketing policy of the two companies. There is no conception of the effects of competition. These students are trying to explain why there are so many different brand names, but only two companies. The important aspect to whether it 'matters' is whether the consumer has enough choice. The D-type conception essentially says that if manufacturers are really producing different sorts of soap powders and not just claiming they are different, then it doesn't matter.

A comparison between the interviews at the beginning and end of the course indicate a clear pattern of students moving to more sophisticated understandings of oligopoly and market competition. So for this concept the course was successful in developing students towards having more sophisticated conceptions of the subject material. However, the pattern of change for the other questions and concepts did not give such an encouraging picture. Although some students developed to more sophisticated understanding of the subject matter, many of them still held the same understanding as at the beginning of the course.

Besides providing insights into the quality of the learning outcomes, a knowledge of students' conceptions of subject materials can form the basis for our teaching. It enables us to start our teaching and training from students' existing understanding of the subject material. This understanding can be especially valuable in open and distance learning, where there may be relatively little opportunity for the face-to-face contact at which you can readily establish students' background knowledge by means of careful questioning.

Some of the research on students' conceptions of capitalism, ie their answers to the question 'Is Britain capitalist?', have been used as a basis for structuring part of the teaching material in the revised course (OU, 1982) The discussion in the text used the responses of the beginning students as the starting point for the teaching so as to help the learner build up to a more sophisticated understanding. If we are aiming to change our students' understanding as a result of our teaching and training, it seems to be crucially important to engage with what our students understand initially so as to facilitate their development of what they understand.

If we return to the example in Chapter 4 of the open learning student, Derek, in general engineering, who referred to the 'black art of electrics' in the interview about his Open Tech course, I think that we can speculate with some degree of confidence, that the course failed to engage with his existing understanding of basic concepts about electricity. He seemed to be constrained by his conception of learning, although aspects of the course design and the teaching could possibly have built on and challenged his prior understanding (and barriers to the subject) and helped him tackle study in a different way – to help foster a deep approach to learning. In open and distance learning formative evaluation (the piloting of teaching and learning materials prior to presentation to students) is often regarded as one of the key stages of course design and course production (see also Thorpe, 1988). However, depending on how the evaluation is carried out, the information and data collected may prove difficult to use for course improvement. It is all too easy to design short questionnaires to elicit students' reponses to teaching materials, but these questions are likely to be framed in terms of the teacher's or trainer's perspectives. There is a need to understand the learner's perspective on the pilot learning materials. In their work for the

Open Tech, Strang and Sagar, (1985) explain how formative evaluation can be frustrating because it just tells us the answers that we would expect. Instead, they suggest that interviews with students are more likely to generate insights into the problems which learners encounter with the materials.

> One-to-one interviews enable the learner's perspective to emerge. Learners decide what to talk about and choose their own dimensions for descriptions . . . quality is more important than quantity. Only interview a handful of learners chosen to represent the different characteristics of your potential learning population. (Strang and Sagar, 1985, p 20)

Also, as we look at how to use research and evaluate data, it takes us back to the notion of the 'reflective practitioner'. Contrary to some of the writings on evaluation, the findings will not provide neat prescriptions which can be implemented; the use of research and evaluation is not a 'technical issue'. Rather the findings can raise awareness of some of the most important issues from the learner's perspective, which contribute to our reflection in action.

The approach outlined above for investigating how people understand aspects of reality, ie, the phenomenographic approach, has been adopted widely in a range of subject areas. Ramsden (1988) summarizes this research in the physical sciences, particularly in physics and chemistry, and how this work has contributed to improving learning, both in schools and at post-compulsory level.

Thinking about your own education and training, are there key concepts which you are attempting to teach your students, but you are not certain about their present understanding of them? If you had the opportunity of a face-to-face tutorial with these students, perhaps you could devise some key questions for them to address, possibly in writing, to be followed with small group discussion, so as to elicit some of the understanding and misunderstanding of your students.

Students' development: skill in learning

How do students come to be more competent and 'better' learners? What are the nature of these changes and how can we facilitate these changes with our students? Students' development of autonomy in learning is one of the aims of post-compulsory education and training, so how do learners describe the changes as they move towards greater independence in learning? These are the questions which are addressed in this section.

So far we have looked at the concepts of outcomes of learning, approaches to learning, conception of learning and orientation to learning as if they are entirely separate. However, if we take a holistic view of the learner engaged in studying, we can see that these concepts are closely interrelated. They provide a set of concepts in increasing level of generality, which form a framework to understanding learning which is firmly grounded in students' realities. We see that students who adopt a deep approach to learning gain a 'good' understanding of the material, the sort which we value in post-compulsory education. In Chapter 3, we saw how different conceptions of learning have a limiting influence on the approach to learning which students adopt. Within the framework presented here the view of 'skill in learning' involves the bringing together of particular intrinsic orientations to study – conceptions of learning described by Säljö as Levels 4 and 5 (learning about constructing meaning and going beyond the information presented) – and adopting a deep approach, thus leading to quality in the learning outcomes. In contrast, students with extrinsic orientations and conceptions of learning concerned with reproducing information (Säljö Levels 1, 2 and 3) will tend to adopt a surface approach to learning, with the corresponding effect on the quality of the learning outcomes. The evidence for the relationships between these concepts has been established by research with OU students (Gibbs, Morgan and Taylor, 1984), which has examined case studies of students over a number of years. Within this framework 'skill in learning' is a relational concept, rather than being concerned with specific techniques which can be isolated from the content of study. As Svensson (1984) explains:

> The term 'study skills' is a common expression which has generally been used to refer to techniques of studying such as notetaking, underlining, summarizing and so on. Interesting as these techniques are, they represent relatively superficial and peripheral aspects of the activity. To see these techniques as skills in themselves is misleading, for this has the effect of isolating them from the student's thinking about the content of the study task of which they form part.

So skill in learning is embedded in engaging actively with learning materials and taking a deep approach, rather than with specific techniques, which can be taught or practised out of the context of the actual content of learning. In terms of improving the quality of our students' learning, we need to help them to adopt a deep approach. In Chapter 5 we saw how various institutional constraints and the impact of the assessment system can easily have unintended side-effects and induce a surface approach to learning.

The importance of orientation to study and how it is related to learning outcomes was also identified by Strang (1987) with students engaged in an Open Tech open learning course. A group of sixteen students, all following the same course, were interviewed so as to understand their orientations to study. Given the nature of the course, students' reasons for studying were primarily vocational. However, there were clear distinctions between those whose orientations were interpreted as intrinsic to the course and those whose orientations were interpreted as extrinsic to the course. In terms of performance on the course as judged by the course assessment, there was a clear link between an intrinsic orientation and gaining the highest grades and students with extrinsic orientations gaining the minimum pass grades. Those with primarily extrinsic orientations were concerned to do the work to pass the assessment, wanted to get the course certificate and saw it as 'completing my qualifications' or 'looking good on my records to impress the boss'. Other students with concerns extrinsic to the course seemed to be studying reluctantly, or had even been told that 'they needed the course certificates to remain in their jobs' and were resentful that passing a course was seen as proof of capability for a job they had been doing for some years. The anxiety and fear of failure which the threat of redundancy is likely to generate is almost certainly going to have an adverse effect on learning for these students.

In contrast, students with a vocational intrinsic orientation saw the content of the course as helpful for their job. Also, following the course provided an opportunity to broaden knowledge about the job and to be able to think more about it in a relaxed context, without the pressures of the actual job. In terms of helping students, it is clearly not really feasible to influence their aims and purposes in study. However, to make them more aware of how they come to be taking a course and what they hope to gain, is likely to make them more reflective about their own attempts at the learning tasks.

To summarize so far, there is a model for understanding student learning, which relates together orientation to education, conception of learning, approach to learning and the quality of the learning outcomes. An important feature of this model is that orientation to education (or a holistic motivation) is related to the context of the adult learner's life, that is, the interactions of study and people's lives in personal and social-political contexts.

Longitudinal studies with OU students (Beaty and Morgan, 1992) in which they were interviewed about their experiences of study every year from their foundation course through to graduation (over a period of six years), identified changes in students which were documented under the three key areas of confidence, competence, and control in learning. One of the main areas where we identified change was when students were asked about learning. Drawing on the work of Säljö, we asked students in each interview the question, 'Can you tell me what you mean by learning?' at an appropriate point in the interview when students described what they had learnt from their current course. The following extracts from the interviews in the first year and the fifth year of study demonstrate the nature of the changes.

> Well I don't know really. I suppose knowing things that I don't know about – I'm still very much at school. I know it's a very different sort of learning and if I look through a book, it's still sort of learning facts and dates and names rather than the content. And if I have read something I'm so bothered about taking in what it said. (Year 1)

> Real learning is something personal and it's also something that is continuous, once it's started, it carries on and on, it might lead to other things. So much learning is learned for a particular purpose, and when you have achieved whatever it was learned for then that's it, it can go away, its disposable, you can get rid of it. But with real learning hopefully the unit of work you are given is only the catalyst really, it is only one hundredth of the learning and the rest goes on once you put the book down. And the next time you talk to someone or read something in the newspaper, that's when the rest happens because it's been started and you carry it on yourself because you want to and you get something lasting. (Year 5)

In this research project with OU students, by the end of their fourth year of study, all the students had developed their conceptions of learning to Säljö's levels 4 or 5. Some of them talked about 'changing as a person' and seeing themselves differently as adult learners in a social and political context.

Students' perceptions of gains from post-compulsory education and training are vitally important for teachers and trainers, especially as there continue to be rapid changes in education and training, both nationally and internationally. Powell (1985) documented what he called the 'residues' of learning, which he gained from autobiographical accounts from graduates about their educational histories, particular the broader gains of academic study, the processes of learning and the formation of attitudes and values. He also identified aspects of students' educational experiences which hindered learning and understanding. In line with other studies, it was found that it was the predominance of overloaded curricula which tended to foster a strategic and mechanistic approach to dealing with assessment demands and 'playing the system'.

So in terms of helping students to develop as learners, we have to enable them to become more aware of how they tackle their studies and open up discussion for them of alternatives (Gibbs, 1981). Enabling students to engage in dialogue, whether in conversation, or through diaries, or even computer-based conferences, is likely to be more successful than any attempt to teach them directly about 'study skills'.

Students' development: autonomy in learning

Another key feature of these research findings is the way students describe changes concerned with the development of independence in learning. Although the students in this study all started in the OU on the social science foundation course, they subsequently followed a wide variety of courses, (mainly social science, arts and technology) so they will have studied courses with quite a variety of structures and pedagogies. The theme of developing independence in learning was clearly identifiable at the interviews. At the beginning of their studies, students tend to be anxious about their capabilities for studying, and assume that they must study all the material in the same detail and also not question the materials. As they develop in confidence and control in their learning, they start to make their own decisions about precisely how to study and also are able to stand back from the content, to relate it to their own aims rather than those of the educational institution. Here is one student in the interview in the first year and the final interview in the sixth year, talking about some of her experiences of studying.

> I got worried at the tutorial because the tutor was picking the unit [correspondence teaching text] to bits and questioning it . . . I said to her, 'Look, I'm a foundation student. I don't pull this unit to bits, I accept what they have told me'. Sometimes I may not like something that is said, but I must accept what is there because I assume they know what they are talking about and if they are putting it to me this way – spoon feeding me – [I am] someone who is unlikely to understand any other way (Year 1).

> I used to think that you had to use your own arguments and I found that very difficult but I know now that you use other people's arguments to build up your own case. So I suppose I have learnt that there are no real right answers and if you get that in your mind to begin with then you can end up agreeing with some theory if you like, but you don't have to . . . It makes you realize that you can take control of your own life. I used to think that life just took hold of you and did what it wanted with you but you come to realize that you should take hold of it and make it go your way (Year 6).

Although there was a significant development in conception of learning, development towards autonomy in learning was not decribed by all the students. The extracts from the interviews above demonstrate the changes for one student. As students develop confidence in studying, so they gain in competence, and these two aspects of change develop side by side. As confidence and competence develop, so the control of learning tends to move from the educational institution (the teacher) and a greater degree of responsibility for it is taken by the student.

Student development of independence and autonomy in learning is an important aim of post-compulsory education and training. In fact a majority of policy statements and reports refer to it. So in Chapter 5 we saw the CNAA and the HMI in the UK calling for greater independence in student learning and less reliance on 'spoon feeding' in formal didactic teaching and the transmission of information. In a similar vein, in the work on capability in education and training, Stephenson (1992) summarizes capability and quality as follows:

> giving students opportunities to be responsible and accountable for their own learning prepares them for effective performance in their personal and working lives, enhances commitment to their studies, promotes deeper understanding, builds confidence in their ability to learn and helps the development of high-level personal qualities and skills. In short, capability education is quality education. (Stephenson, 1992, p 8)

In open learning and distance education there can be ambiguity and problems with the notion of independence in learning. For some people 'independent learning' means the separation of the teacher and the learner, the students working away in isolation at home by themselves. Independence in this sense is the basic feature of distance education. In these terms then, independence may simply mean reducing the amount of academic support through specially prepared study guides or tuition and counselling support, or getting a balance of 'independence and interaction'. There is a considerable literature in distance education, which addresses this theme (eg Daniel and Marquis, 1979; Keegan, 1986).

However, for other people, independent learning is concerned with students taking responsibility for what they learn and how they learn it, developing greater autonomy and self-direction in learning (Percy and Ramsden, 1980; Boud, 1981; Morgan, 1985). In Chapter 5 we saw how aspects of course design and assessment can be used creatively to give students some degree of responsibility in their study through project-based learning, extended essays and assignments which take students outside the immediate realms of what they have been taught. In open and distance learning we need to pay special attention to this, namely, designing scope for student autonomy in learning. As we have already seen, some of the organizational constraints of open and distance learning, with the emphasis on knowledge production and distribution, can lead to the predominance of transmission modes of teaching.

Reflection in learning

What is reflection in learning? I made the case that a basic tenet for improving students' learning is to take account of their experiences; to understand learning from the learner's perspective and to adopt holistic approaches for our research into the student experience and our evaluation of it. In the preceding chapters on students' orientation to education, their conceptions of learning and their approaches to learning, the discussion on how to improve your students' learning has focused on the aspects of our practice which are likely to change and develop students' awareness of how they come to be studying and how they tackle their studies. We saw in Chapter 3 how a student seemed to be caught up by the day-to-day pressures of studying and described herself as 'being on a conveyor'. In terms of improving this student's learning, one aspect of the task is to subject the teaching and especially the assessment procedures to critical scrutiny, both at the level of the individual teacher and trainer and also at an organizational level. The other aspect is to encourage the learner to become more aware of how she came to be engaged in study, her own aims and aspirations, and to help her become more aware of her studying patterns in general.

If we return to the fictional autobiography in Chapter 1, we saw how a change of course resulted in our student tackling study in a very different way from the initial attempts in the first year.

These processes underlying this *change* in awareness can be regarded as 'reflection in learning'. Boud, Keogh and Walker (1985, p19) describe it as follows:

> Reflection in the context of learning is a generic term for those intellectual and affective activities in which individuals engage to explore their experiences in order to lead to new understandings and appreciations. It may take place in isolation or in association with others.

The essence of reflection then is to 'explore experiences and move on to new understandings.' So we can see that for students to develop as learners, they need to move on to new understandings, at the same time as we scrutinize our teaching and learning practice. In examining our practice of teaching and training, I am suggesting that the approach of 'critical reflection', as set out in Chapter 5, is likely to be the most fruitful way to address major change in pedagogy and to understand the barriers and constraints which exist to such change.

Let us look at the notion of reflection-in-learning in more detail. Boud, Keogh and Walker (1985) put particular emphasis on the relationship between the actual learning experience and the learner actively going back to review it. They suggest that there are three key elements to the process of reflection. 'Returning to experience' is the activity of recalling and 'getting back' to whatever learning event we are concerned with – an open learning training package, or a residential school in distance education, for example. 'Attending to feelings' is concerned with exploring the positive and beneficial aspects of that experience, as well as exploring and removing feelings which obstruct further consideration of the learning experience. This leads on to the third element of 're-evaluating experience', which involves examining the experience in the light of the learners' intentions, exploring new knowledge relating this to existing knowledge, and building up to the learners' existing conceptual framework. Although these three elements are described separately, they tend to overlap in practice, and are not to be regarded as strictly distinct. Also given the cyclical nature of the three elements of this model, learners may well go through a number of cycles.

There are some similarities to the model of experiential learning set out by Kolb and Fry (1975) This is a four-stage model, which stresses the importance of experience in the learning process: (i) the immediate concrete learning experience is the starting point, which is the basis for (ii), reflection and observation; (iii) these reflections and observations are incorporated into the existing understanding (or theory) and (iv) the incorporation of these observations leads to new implications and active experimentation. Kolb argues that the four stages are required for learners to be effective. (See Gibbs (1988) for an elaboration of the Kolb experiential learning cycle.)

The notion of reflection in learning seems applicable to education and training in a wide range of contexts. For example, Boud and Walker (1991) adopted the approach as a key part of an industrial training programme for a newly promoted production supervisor. Rather than viewing the training programme as a discrete event for the trainee, the learner was encouraged to continue working from the training programme as the basis for reviewing her experiences in her new more senior position as supervisor. She worked with a diary to record experiences of learning in the workplace and how her formal learning related to the day-to-day demands of the job. So, through the process of reflection, she was able to become more aware of herself in the organization and the constraints she had to operate under. Reflection after the experience is an essential activity for becoming aware of the personal, political and social dimensions to the learning process.

If we look at the learning process in a broader context, we see a complex pattern of the interactions of studying with people's lives. These interactions can have a major impact for adult learners, particularly part-time students, where learning can contribute to major adult change and development. If we look at learning outcomes from the learners' perspectives in these terms, we gain different insights into students' perceptions of gains from study.

In a preliminary analysis of student interviews in a longitudinal study of OU student learning (Holly and Morgan, 1992) one of the key themes emerging was the way in which the relationships with partners impinged on OU study. The impact of study for some students created a polarization in their domestic household units. One of these themes was labelled 'education without consent'. This was a crucial factor in the experience of being a student for some of the women interviewed in this study. They received no support or encouragement from their partners. Their study was like a sort of clandestine 'relationship', and studying was constrained by the sexual division of labour within the household – they were still required to fulfil the conventional domestic demands of providing meals, etc. Studying was almost done in 'secret', when the husband was out of the house. Another woman gave a vivid account of how she disguised the course units inside popular magazines, so that she could read them in the living room while the husband watched television.

These women experience hostility from their husbands, who feel threatened and intellectually insecure. They face a dilemma as they are confronted with a choice between supporting a relationship with the husband or the intellectual development to be gained through study. So we can see another crucial dimension to understanding the outcomes of learning when we take account of the learners' experiences.

Commentary

In this chapter, we have looked at how students change and develop as a result of their studies. As soon as we move on from a quantitative notion for understanding learning, we see the complexity of the learning process. However, by gaining valuable descriptions from the learners' perspective, as teacher, trainers and course designers in open and distance learning, we shall be in a better position to theorize our practice, so as to improve learning for our students.

Chapter 7

Conclusions: research, theory and practice

In this final chapter, I want to draw together the conclusions from the fore-going chapters and summarize the implications of this work for teachers, trainers and course designers, as a brief commentary on research, theory and practice in open and distance learning. The thesis of this book is that if we are to take our efforts to improve students' learning seriously, we need to take account of learning from the learner's perspective. In looking at the learners' experiences of studying, the conceptual framework has been developed which relates together the five dimensions of orientation to education, conception of learning, approach to learning, the outcomes of learning, and aspects of course design and assessment. So for improving students' learning, we need to concentrate our attention on helping students to adopt a deep approach to learning.

On the one hand then, we have to help students become more aware of how they come to be engaged in study, and enable them to articulate their orientations to education and training, as well as help them develop their conceptions of learning. And on the other hand, we have to take a critical look at our course design and assessment practices. The importance of this conceptual framework is that the concept of orientation to education (discussed in Chapter 2) can be seen as the link between the more detailed processes of studying and the social and political context of learners' lives. This conceptual framework or model can be regarded as a theory based on orientation, conception of learning and approach to learning. By using the term theory here, I am using it in the sense of searching for and describing the key issues and concepts of teaching and learning, and attempting to identify the relationships between them, rather than in the sense of hypothesis testing, as in the physical sciences. This theoretical framework suggests that change in students' orientations and change and development in their conceptions of learning will lead them to adopt a deep approach to their learning.

Within this framework for understanding and improving students' learning, skill in learning is concerned with the interrelationship of orientation, conception of learning and a deep approach to learning, rather than with specific techniques which can be taught and practised out of context of the content of study. Where we are in a position to develop some face-to-face contact with our students in open and distance learning, the structured discussions as described by Gibbs (1981) can be an excellent approach for helping students to develop their awareness as the basis for change.

As well as helping students change in how they tackle their studies, the other crucial aspect for improving student learning is institutional change and the development of our teaching and learning practices. In Chapters 4 and 5 we saw how certain aspects of course design and assessment can induce students to adopt a surface approach to their learning, with the corresponding influence on the quality of the learning outcomes. As well as working on developing course design and assessment, we also need to ensure that research and evaluation in open and distance learning is carried out to describe students' experiences of novel and creative approaches to our practice.

In conducting these research and evaluation studies, it is important that the studies are designed to build on and extend existing research, so that there is a cumulative development of understanding of teaching and learning in open and distance learning, and subsequently further development of theory. It will be clear to you by now that the majority of the research which has been referred to in this book has been conducted with qualitative research methodologies, in most cases with individual in-depth interviews. However, I do not want to set up any sort of polarization between qualitative and quantitative research methods. On the contrary, there is a need for a complementarity of methodologies to address the problems of student learning in open and distance learning. The key factor is that research and evaluation studies should build on each other so as to lead to cumulative development of our understanding. The methodological perspective adopted in much of the research in this book is summarized succinctly by Säljö (1988, p 35), as follows:

> It is the basic tenet that there is no necessary conflict between qualitative and quantitative approaches for generating and analysing data. Indeed, it is highly questionable whether it is meaningful at all to argue about

method without simultaneously considering the research problem one is facing and the knowledge interest being pursued. Given the conception of learning . . . it is evident that a family of methods conventionally referred to as qualitative is of primary importance. A thorough understanding of what learning means in concrete terms in various settings presupposes a detailed analysis of how students deal with the tasks they are presented . . . In saying this we are trying to establish another fundamental assumption behind the research into everyday human learning . . . Access to *the learners' perspective* on the activities of teaching and learning is essential for understanding educational phenomena . . . and for improving education.

If we have been able to generate insights into learning from the learners' perspective, this begs another question: how do we use the research finding? At one level, this could be regarded as feedback from the learners, which will subsequently influence course design and course improvement. This is the conventional systems approach to educational technology, which assumes that a teaching and learning system will behave as a rational feedback model, reacting and responding to feedback. Although this model may be attractive, in practice the real world is very different. Donald Schon (1983) is critical of what he calls the 'technical rationality', or the official scientific view of how professionals are supposed to act, as a totally inadequate description. He sets out the notion of 'reflection in action' as a more realistic model for understanding professional practice, which acknowledges judgement and the interpretation of research. Reflection-in-action implies that the practitioner becomes a 'researcher' of that practice, as he or she is required to make sense of and understand new situations. This requires the practitioner to be reflective, as a key to understanding unexpected and novel situations.

As I am writing from an organizational base in the Institute of Educational Technology at the Open University, it seems appropriate to examine the content and approach of this book in relation to educational technology and likely changes in this field. I suggest that 'traditional educational technology' and the way that feedback and change in teaching and learning are conceived of are no longer adequate for understanding the realities of how teachers, trainers and course designers operate as practitioners. The rational models of organizational change are being replaced or modified by an understanding of the process in terms of cultural and political views, which acknowledge the existence of contestation and the micro-politics and sub-cultures within organizations (Pettigrew, 1985). I detect an emerging pattern within the field which recognizes reflectivity in educational technology beyond the boundaries of the rationalist model, which is concerned with a much broader level of *change* in education and *change* in society. I suggest that a 'new educational technology' can be considered as focusing on three crucial levels of *change*.

- Change from the learners' perspective, looking at outcomes of learning, students' development, and the interactions of learning with people's lives.
- Organizational change, concerned with our teaching, learning and assessment practice, and our pedagogy; whom we teach, and a concern for issues of access and equal opportunity.
- Change in education and training within the overall social and economic climate, and change in open and distance learning, in a rapidly changing international context.

These three levels of change are closely interrelated, but offer a much wider understanding of educational technology than is conventionally conceived of, within its origins in programmed learning and instructional technology.

In looking at emerging trends in educational technology, evaluation is one area where there have been important changes over the last decade or so. Malcolm Parlett has been influential in placing illuminative evaluation on the agenda (Parlett and Hamilton, 1977), as an approach to evaluation which goes beyond the physical science models for attempting to understand the complexities of educational programmes. Illuminative evaluation is concerned with description and documentation, so as to find out 'what is really going on' in a complex setting, in contrast to attempting to adopt precise techniques for measurement. Parlett (1991) draws on the work of Kurt Lewin (1952) in stressing the importance of holistic approaches for understanding complex phenomena:

> We live at a time of unprecedented activity and innovation, in which new thinking is being applied to many areas of science and human effort. There are moves towards more holistic approaches, more relativistic outlooks, and there is more reflexivity regarding the role of the observer; interdependent relationships are more widely acknowledged, and the limitations of applying mechanical-type thinking to areas beyond engineering are more frequently acknowledged (Parlett, 1991, p 75).

The key point here is the limits to mechanistic models for understanding complex social phenomena. Although Parlett was writing in the context of gestalt psychotherapy, the work of Lewin forms part of the basis of contemporary 'action research' and critical reflection (Carr and Kemmis, 1986;

Kemmis, 1985; Evans and Nation, 1989b). The approach of 'critical reflection' is introduced above, particularly in Chapter 5, in looking at the organizational context of learning and the details of teaching and assessment practices. Throughout this book, the aim has been to provide holistic understandings of learner's experience of learning.

Finally, what are the key implications of the research in the foregoing chapters for informing our practice in open and distance learning? In Chapters 4 and 6 we discussed some of the attempts which have been made to help students adopt a deep approach to learning. The aim is to encourage students to engage actively with the learning materials. However, we saw that some of the efforts to manipulate student learning can easily induce students to take a surface approach. The challenge is to design learning activities which actively engage students in dialogue, and also involve them in taking some degree of control and responsibility for their learning. We saw how project-based learning is one possible way to involve students in their learning. Throughout this book, I have drawn attention to the power of the assessment system for influencing how students are required to tackle their studies, and how frequently much of the assessment demands little more than reproducing information. The consequence of this is that students adopt a surface approach to their learning. Similarly, excessive workloads will tend to foster surface approaches, as due to the sheer volume of what students are expected to cope with, they will end up having to make relatively arbitrary guesses about which parts of the curriculum to concentrate on. Ramsden (1992, p 178), summarized the tasks for improving learning as follows:

> [The task] is to discourage students from using surface approaches: this implies avoiding excessive workloads, busywork, and unnecessary time pressures; shunning assessment practices that require recall or rehearsal of trivial detail; abandoning all attempts to devalue students' tentative steps towards understanding; avoiding cynical comments (explicit or implicit) about the subject matter and students' grasp of it.

Although these remarks are directed at teachers in conventional educational settings, they seem to be equally pertinent to education and training in open and distance learning.

As we theorize our practice, we need to be aware of how aspects of course design and assessment and the 'hidden curriculum' can so easily induce students to adopt a surface approach. The challenge for us in open and distance learning is to design our learning activities so as to engage our students in dialogue. Also when students take some degree of control and responsibility for their learning and participate more in the processes of learning and teaching, they are more likely to adopt a deep approach to their learning. If we can achieve this, then the quality in the learning outcomes and students' experiences of learning will be significantly enhanced.

References

Altrichter, H, Evans, T D and Morgan, A R (1991) *Windows: Research and Evaluation on a Distance Education Course*, Geelong, Australia: Deakin University Press.

Beaty, L (formerly Taylor) (1987) 'Understanding concepts in social science: towards an effective evaluation strategy', *Instructional Science*, **15**, pp 341–59.

Beaty, L and Morgan, A R (1992) 'Developing skill in learning', *Open Learning*, **7**, 3, pp 3–11.

Becker, H, Geer, B and Hughes, EC (l968) *Making the Grade – the Academic Side of College Life*, New York: Wiley.

Belenky, M F, Clinchy, B M, Goldberger, N R and Tarule, J M (1986) *Women's Ways of Knowing*. New York: Basic Books.

Black, H and Wolf, A (1990) (eds) *Knowledge and Competence*, Careers and Occupational Information Centre, HMSO.

Boud, D (1981) (ed) *Developing Student Autonomy in Learning*, London: Kogan Page.

Boud, D, Keogh, R and Walker, D (1985) (eds) *Reflection: Turning Experience in Learning*, London: Kogan Page.

Boud, D and Walker, D (1991) *Experience and Learning: Reflection at Work*, Geelong, Australia: Deakin University Press.

Brown, G (1991) *Competence and Assessment*, **17**, pp 11–15.

Campion, M (1990) 'Post-Fordism and research in distance education' in Evans, T D (ed) *Research in Distance Education*, **I**, Geelong, Australia: Deakin University Press.

Carr, W and Kemmis, S (1986) *Becoming Critical: Education, Knowledge and Action Research*, Lewes: Falmer Press.

Chambers, E (1992) 'Work-load and the quality of student learning', *Studies in Higher Education*, **17**, 2, pp 141–53.

Clarke, B and Trow, M (l966) 'The organisational context', in Newcombe, T M and Wilson, E K (eds) *College Peer Groups*, Chicago: Aldine.

Dahlgren, L O (1975) 'Qualitative differences in learning as a function of content-oriented guidance', *Göteborg Studies in Educational Sciences*, **15**, Gothenburg: Acta Universitatis Gothoburgensis.

Dahlgren, L O and Marton, F (1978) 'Students' conceptions of subject matter: an aspect of learning and teaching in higher education', *Studies in Higher Education*, **3**, pp 25–35.

Dahlgren, L O (1984) 'Outcomes of Learning' in Marton, F, Hounsell, D and Entwistle, N (eds) *The Experience of Learning*, Edinburgh: Scottish Academic Press.

Daniel, J and Marquis, C (1979) 'Interaction and independence: getting the mixture right', *Teaching at a Distance*, **15**, pp 25–44.

Entwistle, A and Entwistle, N (1992) 'Experiences of understanding in revising for degree examination', *Learning and Instruction*, **2**, 1, pp 1–22.

Entwistle, N and Ramsden, P (1983) *Understanding Student Learning*, London: Croom Helm.

Eraut, M (1990) 'Identifying the knowledge which underpins performance', in Black, H and Wolf, A (eds) *Knowledge and Competence*, Careers and Occupational Information Centre, HMSO.

Evans, T D (1991) 'An epistemological orientation to critical reflection in distance education', in Evans, T D and King, B (eds) *Beyond the Text*, Geelong, Australia: Deakin University Press.

Evans, T D and Nation, D (1989a) 'Dialogue in the theory, practice and research of distance education', *Open Learning*, **4**, 2, pp 37–46.

Evans, T D and Nation, D E (eds) (1989b) *Critical Reflections on Distance Education*, Lewes: Falmer Press.

Farnes, N (1993) 'Modes of production and stages of educational development: Fordism and distance education', *Open Learning*, **8**, 1 (in press).

Freire, P (1972) *Pedagogy of the Oppressed*, Harmondsworth: Penguin.

Gibbs, G (1981) *Teaching Students to Learn*, Milton Keynes: Open University Press.

Gibbs, G (1988) *Learning by Doing*, London: Further Education Unit.

Gibbs, G (1992) *Improving the Quality of Student Learning*. Bristol: Technical and Educational Services Ltd.

Gibbs, G, Morgan, A and Taylor, E (1982) 'Why students don't learn', *Institutional Research Review*, **1**, pp 9–32.

Gibbs, G, Morgan, A R and Taylor, E (1984) 'The world of the learner', in Marton, F, Entwistle, N and Hounsell, D (eds) *The Experience of Learning*, Edinburgh: Scottish Academic Press.

Giddens, A (1976) *New Rules of Sociological Method*, London: Hutchinson.

Giddens, A (1984) *The Constitution of Society*, Cambridge: Polity Press.

Goodson, I and Walker, R (1988) 'Putting life into educational research' in Sherman, R R and Webb, R B (eds), *Qualitative Research in Education: Focus and Methods*, Lewes: Falmer Press.

Goodyear, M (1975) 'A study of motivation at the Open University', London:

Market Behaviour Ltd, commissioned by the Institute of Educational Technology, Open University.

Habeshaw, T, Habeshaw, S and Gibbs, G (1987) *53 Interesting Ways of Helping Your Students to Study*, Bristol: Technical and Educational Services Ltd.

Harris, D (1987) *Openness and Closure in Distance Education*, Lewes: Falmer Press.

Harris, D and Holmes, J (1976) 'Openness and control in higher education: towards a critique of the Open University', in Dale, R, Esland, G and MacDonald, M (eds) *Schooling and Capitalism*, London: Routledge.

HMI (1990) 'The English Polytechnics'.

Holly, L and Morgan, A R (1993) 'Education without consent', *Student Research Centre Report*, **73**, Milton Keynes: Institute of Educational Technology, Open University.

Holt, D, Petzall, S and Viljoen, J (1990) 'The MBA experience by distance learning: what MBA participants bring to their studies', *Open Learning*, **5**, 3, pp 16–27.

Jeffcoate, R (1981) 'Why can't a unit be more like a book?' *Teaching at a Distance*, **20**, pp 75–6.

Keegan, D (1986) *Foundations of Distance Education*, London: Croom Helm (2nd edition, 1990, London: Routledge).

Kemmis, S (1985) 'Action research and the politics of reflection', in Boud, D, Keogh, R and Walker, D (eds), *Reflection: Turning Experience into Learning*, London: Kogan Page.

Laurillard, D (1979) 'The processes of learning', *Higher Education*, **8**, pp 395–409.

Leigh, A (1992) 'The assessment of vocational and academic competence', *Competence and Assessment,* (Journal of the Employment Department's Standards Methodology Branch), **17**, pp 18–20.

Lewin, K (1952) *Field Theory in Social Science*, London: Tavistock.

Lockwood, F (1992) *Activities in Self-Instructional Texts*, London: Kogan Page.

Lodge, D (1975) *Changing Places*, Harmondsworth: Penguin Books.

Marton, F (1981) 'Phenomenography – describing conceptions of the world around us', *Instructional Science*, **10**, pp 117–200.

Marton, F, Dall'Alba, G and Beaty, E (1993) 'Conceptions of learning', *International Journal of Educational Research*, (in press).

Marton, F, Hounsell, D and Entwistle, N (eds) (1984), *The Experience of Learning*, Edinburgh: Scottish Academic Press.

Marton, F and Säljö, R (1976) 'On qualitative differences, outcomes and process I and II', *British Journal of Educational Psychology*, **46**, pp 4–11, 115–127.

Marton, F and Säljö, R (1979) 'Learning in the learner's perspective III: Level of difficulty seen as a relationship between the reader and the text', *Report No 78*, Institute of Education, University of Gothenburg.

Marton, F and Säljö, R (1984) 'Approaches to learning', in Marton, F, Hounsell, D and Entwistle, N (eds) *The Experience of Learning*, Edinburgh: Scottish Academic Press.

Meek, V L (1983) *The Gippsland Institute: A Sociological Case Study of a Regional College of Advanced Education*, Melbourne: University of Melbourne Centre for the Study of Higher Education.

Miller, C & Parlett, M (1974) *Up to the Mark: A Study of the Examination Game*, Guildford: Society for Research in Higher Education.

Morgan, A R (1983) 'Theoretical aspects of project-based learning in higher education', *British Journal of Educational Technology*, **14**, 1, pp 66–78.

Morgan, A R (1984) *Students' and Tutors' Experiences of Project Work*, Report for Educational Methods Unit, Oxford Polytechnic.

Morgan, A R (1985) 'What shall we do about independent learning?', *Teaching at a Distance*, **26**, 38–45.

Morgan, A R (1988) 'Course design and students' approaches to study', in Sewart, D and Daniel, J S (eds), *Developing Distance Education*, Oslo: International Council of Distance Education.

Morgan, A R (1988) 'Students' experiences of study: M205 The fundamentals of computing', *Student Research Centre Report* **28**, Milton Keynes: Institute of Educational Technology, Open University.

Morgan, A R, Gibbs, G and Taylor, L (1980) 'Students' approaches to studying the social science and technology foundation courses', *Study Methods Group Report* **4**, Milton Keynes: Institute of Educational Technology, Open University.

Morgan, A. R, Gibbs, G and Taylor, E (1981) 'What do Open University students initially understand about learning?', *Study Methods Group Report* **8**, Milton Keynes: Institute of Educational Technology, Open University.

Morgan, A R, Taylor, E and Gibbs, G (1982) 'Variations in students' approaches to studying', *British Journal of Educational Technology*, **13**, 2, pp 107–13.

Morgan, A R and Thorpe, M (1993) 'Residential schools in distance education: quality time for quality learning?' in Evans, T D and Nation, D (eds), *Reforming Open Learning and Distance Education*, London: Kogan Page.

Nation, D (1991) 'Teaching texts and independent learning', in Evans, T D and King, B (eds), *Beyond the Text*, Geelong, Australia: Deakin University Press.

Open University (1982) 'The economy: A social process', Unit 5, Social Science Foundation Course (D102). Milton Keynes: Open University.

Parlett, M (1977) 'The learning milieu', *Studies in Higher Education*, **2** 2, pp 173–181.

Parlett, M (1991) 'Reflections on field theory', *British Gestalt Journal*, **1**, 2, pp 69–81.

Parlett, M and Hamilton, D (1977) 'Evaluation as illumination', in Hamilton, D, Jenkins, D, King, C, MacDonald, B and Parlett, M (eds), *Beyond the Numbers Game*, Basingstoke: Macmillan.

Percy, K and Ramsden, P (1980) *Independent Study: Two Examples from English Higher Education*, Guildford: Society for Research in Higher Education.

Perry, W G (1970) *Forms of Intellectual and Ethical Development in the College Years: A Scheme*, New York: Holt, Rinehart and Winston.

Pettigrew, A W (1985) *The Awakening Giant: Continuity and Change in Imperial Chemical Industries*, Oxford: Blackwell.

Powell, J P (1985) 'The residues of learning: Autobiographical accounts by graduates of the impact of higher education', *Higher Education*, **14**, 127–47.

Ramsden, P (ed) (1988) *Improving Learning: New Perspectives*, London: Kogan Page.

Ramsden, P (1992) *Learning to Teach in Higher Education*, London: Routledge.

Rickards, J P and Denner, P R (1978) 'Inserted questions as aids to reading texts', *Instructional Science*, **7**, pp 313–46.

Rogers, C (1969) *Freedom to Learn*. Columbus, Ohio: Merrill.

Rowntree, D (1977) *Assessing Students: How Shall We know Them?* London: Harper and Row.

Rowntree, D (1982) *Curriculum Development and Educational Technology*, 2nd edition, London: Harper and Row.

Rowntree, D (1985) *Developing Courses for Students*, London: Harper and Row.

Rowntree, D (1988) *Learn How to Study*, London: Macdonald Orbis.

Rowntree, R (1992) *Exploring Open and Distance Learning*, London: Kogan Page.

Russell, Willy (1986) *Educating Rita*, London: Methuen.

Sagar, E and Strang, A (1985) *The Student Experience*, London: HMSO and Cambridge: National Extension College.

Säljö, R. (1979) 'Learning about learning', *Higher Education*, **8**, pp 443–51.

Säljö R. (1982) 'Learning and understanding', *Göteborg Studies in Educational Science* **41**, Gothenburg: Acta Universitatis Gothoburgensis.

Säljö, R (1988) 'Learning in educational settings: methods of inquiry' in Ramsden, P (ed) *Improving Learning: New Perspectives*, London: Kogan Page.

Schon, D (1973) *Beyond the Stable State*, Harmondsworth: Pelican Books.

Schon, D (1983) *The Reflective Practitioner: How Professionals think in action* London: Temple Smith.

Schon, D (1987) *Educating the Reflective Practitioner*, San Francisco: Jossey-Bass.

Snyder, B (1971) *The Hidden Curriculum*, New York: Knopf.

Stephenson, J (1992) 'Capability and quality in higher education', in Stephenson, J and Weil, S (eds), *Quality in Learning*, London: Kogan Page.

Strang, A (1987) 'The Hidden Barriers', in Hodgson, V E, Mann, S J and Snell, R (eds), *Beyond Distance Teaching – Towards Open Learning*, Milton Keynes: Society for Research in Higher Education & Open University Press.

Strang, A and Sagar, E (1985) *Using the Learner's Perspective. Materials Design for Effective Open Learning*, Cambridge: National Extension College.

Student Research Centre (1986) 'The human dimension in Open University Study', *Open Learning*, **1**, 2, pp 14–17.

Svensson, L (1984) 'Skill in learning', in Marton, F, Entwistle, N and Hounsell, D (eds), *The Experience of Learning*, Edinburgh: Scottish Academic Press.

Tavistock Institute of Human Relations (1990) *The First Year of Enterprise in Higher Education*, Sheffield: Employment Department.

Taylor, E (1983) 'Orientations to study: a longitudinal interview investigation of students in two human studies degree courses at Surrey University', PhD thesis, Guildford: University of Surrey. (Taylor is now named Beaty.)

Taylor, E, Gibbs, G and Morgan, A R (1980) 'The orientations of students studying the Social Science Foundation Course', *Study Methods Group Report* **7**, Milton Keynes: Institute of Educational Technology, Open University.

Taylor, E, Gibbs, G, and Morgan, A R (1981) 'The outcomes of learning from the social science foundation course: students' understandings of price control, power and oligopoly', *Study Methods Group Report* **9**, Milton Keynes: Institute of Educational Technology, Open University.

Taylor, E, Morgan, A R and Gibbs, G (1981) *Teaching at a Distance*, **20**, pp 3–12.

Thorpe, M (1988) *Evaluating Open and Distance Learning*, Harlow: Longmans.

van Rossum, E J and Schenk, S M (1984) 'The relationship between learning conception, study strategy and learning outcome', *British Journal of Educational Psychology*, **54**, pp 73–83.

Index